C000226266

THE GORDON HIGHLANDERS

Also by Trevor Royle in the same series

The Royal Scots

The Black Watch

The Royal Highland Fusiliers

Queen's Own Highlanders

THE GORDON HIGHLANDERS

A Concise History

TREVOR ROYLE

EDINBURGH AND LONDON

Copyright © Trevor Royle, 2007
All rights reserved
The moral right of the author has been asserted

First published in Great Britain in 2007 by
MAINSTREAM PUBLISHING COMPANY
(EDINBURGH) LTD
7 Albany Street
Edinburgh EH1 3UG

ISBN 9781845962708

No part of this book may be reproduced or transmitted in any form or by any other means without permission in writing from the publisher, except by a reviewer who wishes to quote brief passages in connection with a review written for insertion in a magazine, newspaper or broadcast

A catalogue record for this book is available
from the British Library

Typeset in Bembo

Printed in Great Britain by
William Clowes Ltd, Beccles, Suffolk

Contents

Preface

The Gordon Highlanders disappeared from the British Army's Order of Battle in 1994 following the amalgamation with Queen's Own Highlanders to form The Highlanders (Seaforth, Gordons and Camerons). Twelve years later there was an even more fundamental change when The Highlanders became the 4th battalion of The Royal Regiment of Scotland, the new 'large' regiment formed as a result of radical reforms in the structure of the British infantry. Inevitably the changes created a great deal of sadness in the army community and more widely throughout Scotland, with regret being expressed for the loss of some cherished names and the conversion of regiments into a new formation. However, the history of the British Army shows that the story of its regiments has been one of constant development, with cutbacks, amalgamations and changes of name being part of a process of evolution stretching back over several centuries. In every case the development has not led to a diminution of the army's capabilities but has produced new regiments that are the equal of their predecessors.

Together with the other books in the series, this concise history has been written to mark this latest transformation in Scottish and

British military history. As the Gordons shared their story with Queen's Own Highlanders between 1994 and 2006 the final pages of this account are common to both histories. This is not a new regimental history of the regiment and its predecessors, but I hope it will be a useful addition to the regiment's historiography. Invariably, as is the case with the other concise regimental histories, it also reflects the history of the British Army and the empire in which it served. I owe a tremendous debt to previous regimental historians, whose books are listed in the bibliography. It goes without saying, I hope, that the history of the regiment could not have been attempted without a thorough reading of the six volumes of *Life of a Regiment,* which traces the history of the Gordons from its beginnings in 1787 to 1970.

I am grateful to the following for granting permission to quote from copyright material: Philip Carson for permission to quote from the private papers of Lieutenant-Colonel R.A. Wolfe Murray DSO, MC; Cath Scott for permission to quote from 'Coronach For the Dead of the 5/7th Battalion The Gordon Highlanders' by Alexander Scott MC, from Alexander Scott, *Selected Poems 1943–1974,* Akros Publications, Preston, 1975.

For help throughout the project I would like to thank Lieutenant-Colonel Alastair Cumming, the Regimental Secretary of The Highlanders until 2006. At the Gordon Highlanders Museum in Aberdeen (an excellent example of its kind) I owe a debt of gratitude to the curator Sarah Malone for her help and support, and I want to thank Stewart Mitchell, Debbie Perry, Charles Reid and Major Malcolm Ross who gave unstinting assistance in the selection of illustrations. Grateful thanks are also due to Brigadier the Hon. Hugh B.H.E. Monro who gave his blessing to the project during his period of office as Colonel of The Highlanders.

Trevor Royle

ONE

A Gordon for Me

For two centuries, from its foundation in 1794 to its amalgamation with Queen's Own Highlanders in 1994 to form The Highlanders, The Gordon Highlanders was one of the best-known regiments in the British Army. It recruited mainly from the north-east of Scotland and its personality was formed from the fishing and farming communities which give the area its character – tough, unyielding, reticent of speech and blessed by an idiosyncratic sense of humour. A total of 18 Victoria Crosses were won by Gordon Highlanders, its battle honours are a roll-call of campaigns fought by the British Army over two centuries and the distinctive yellow stripe in its government tartan kilt was widely known and respected. It also gave the army some of its finest soldiers, amongst whom may be mentioned Field Marshal George White, the winner of a Victoria Cross in 1879 and General Sir Ian Hamilton, the commander of the ill-fated Gallipoli campaign in 1915, who was allegedly twice turned down for the same award, on the first occasion because he was considered to be too young and the second because he was too senior. Another fine and upstanding

Gordon Highlander was Major-General Sir Hector Macdonald, who rose from the ranks, an unusual achievement, to become one of the best-known soldiers of the late Victorian period. And in more recent times the regiment was memorialised in the fictional Private McAuslan stories written by George Macdonald Fraser, the creator of the Flashman novels, who himself served in the 2nd battalion immediately after the Second World War. The regiment also gave rise to a popular music-hall ditty composed by Robert Wilson in which 'Geordie Mackay of the HLI' is rejected while courting because he serves in the wrong regiment. The girl's catchy response in the chorus says it all:

> A Gordon for me, a Gordon for me,
> If ye're no' a Gordon, ye're no use to me.
> The Black Watch are braw, the Seaforth an' a',
> But the cocky wee Gordon's the pride o' them a'.

Also inspired by the regiment was the catchphrase 'the Gordons will take it' which enjoyed a wide currency at the end of the nineteenth century. During the storming of the Heights of Dargai in 1897 in India's North-West Frontier Province Piper George Findlater won a gallant Victoria Cross (see Chapter Five) while continuing to play the pipes even though he had been wounded in both legs. The action was widely reported, turning the piper into a national hero. At the same time the commanding officer's words before battle also entered the national consciousness. Told that his regiment had to capture the position, Lieutenant-Colonel H.H. Mathias responded with the immortal words: 'The General [Sir William Lockhart] says this hill must be taken at all costs – the Gordon Highlanders will take it.' Soon wags in London clubs were saying that the same thing would happen if anyone left an umbrella unattended – 'the Gordons will take it'. And yet, the history of the regiment is not just about The Gordon Highlanders. It also embraces another fine regiment, the 75th Highlanders, with which it was amalgamated in 1881 during one of the army's many periods of reform. The 75th was designated the Stirlingshire Regiment and although it had a distinguished record of service it more or less disappeared from history and very little is known about its foundation or its antecedents. At the time of the amalgamation the 75th had already lost its Highland status and although it became the 1st battalion of the new regiment, it is fair to say that when The Gordon Highlanders came into being it was not so much an amalgamation of equals as a takeover by the younger regiment.

The 75th Highlanders was formed in 1787 and, in common with the other Highland regiments raised during this period, its existence owed everything to Prince Charles Edward Stewart's Jacobite rebellion of 1745–46 and the government's response to it. In the aftermath of the defeat of the Jacobite army at Culloden the government forces commanded by the Duke of Cumberland had indulged in atrocity and summary justice as they set about rounding up the Jacobite rebels and pacifying the heartland which had supported them. The duke's policy was 'to bruise those bad seeds spread about this country so as they might never shoot again' and, in so doing, to prevent the Highlands from offering their traditional threat to the body politic. It was a chance, he said, to demonstrate to the clans that they were not above the law and that it was in the power of the government's security forces to march into lands previously considered inaccessible in order to pacify the inhabitants. The clans were forced to disarm, their centres of power were destroyed – around 7,000 houses were razed and steps were taken to position garrisons throughout the Highlands. Finally, measures were introduced for 'disarming and undressing those savages' through the Disarming Act of August 1746. Not only were traditional weapons and the plaid made illegal, but Highlanders were forced to swear an oath of allegiance which left the clansman in no doubt that his day was over. The act was not repealed until 1782, but by that time it had achieved its main objective.

The destruction of Highland Scottish military power and the Clearances of the traditional clan lands which accompanied it was a watershed in Scotland's history. Not only was it the beginning of the end of a way of life which was barely understood by outsiders, but it changed for ever the complexion of the Highlands and Gaelic cultural life. Later the Clearances came to be remembered as a shameful period, with its forced evictions, as people made way for the cultivation of sheep, but at the time the process was largely welcomed. In addition to improving their own financial situation, many landowners genuinely believed that they were helping their tenants to create better lives for themselves. Besides, in the aftermath of the union of the parliaments in 1707 and the resultant economic benefits of 'heavenly Hanoverianism', it was thought no bad thing to have this lawless area, with its savage population brought under control. What to do with it was another matter. Either the Highlanders could accept modernity and the union or they could be moved elsewhere, and many Highland landowners claimed that they were merely improving the lot of their tenants by encouraging them to move to new lives in the New World. As for the soldierly instincts of the menfolk, these could be offered to the British Army at a time when there was a constant need for recruits.

In fact, steps had already been taken to channel Highland militarism into the service of the state, with the creation of six Independent Companies of the Highland Watch in 1725. These paramilitary police units had been brought into being earlier in the century as small independent companies to prevent smuggling and generally to help keep the peace in the areas where the

Lowlands gave way to the Highlands. They had been a mixed success, being irregular forces with a poor command structure, but the creation of these 'watches' represented a breakthrough; in 1739 another four companies were added and the new formation was given the status of a regiment of the line, as the 43rd Highland Regiment of Foot. Later it became better known as The Black Watch or Royal Highland Regiment and was renumbered 42nd. But it was during the Seven Years War (1756–63) that the prime minister, William Pitt the Elder, opened the door for the creation of the Highland regiments. Highlanders were regarded as good soldiers, their powers of endurance and fighting qualities were well known and, being members of clans, they would bring with them a sense of coherence and loyalty which would translate into good military practice. As the days of the clan system were numbered after Culloden and would soon disappear, other than as sentimental entities based on chiefdoms, tartans and yearning for a lost past, the Highland regiments became handy substitutes.

Not that the creation of the Highland regiments was universally popular, either in England or in Scotland. Memories of Highland violence and savagery were still vivid, but Pitt insisted that the recruitment of the Highlanders served two purposes – a steady supply of good soldiers for service in Europe, North America and India and a means of finally pacifying a previously troublesome area by ridding it of its warlike young men. If they were killed on active service, then that might be no bad thing either: it was clear that many Highlanders would not return to their native lands, especially if they were fighting in colonial wars. And if the policy of raising the regiments was intended to complete the depopulation of the Highlands, the fighting in America certainly helped the process. Once their regiments were disbanded, as happened on a regular basis at the end of any conflict, it was hoped that many Highland soldiers would simply settle in America, where they would provide a loyal bulwark against any secession movement. In 1766 Pitt defended in parliament his decision to raise the Highland regiments:

> I have no local attachments: it is indifferent to me, whether a man was rocked in his cradle on this side or that of the Tweed. I sought for merit wherever it was to be found. It is my boast, that I was the first minister who looked for it, and I found it in the mountains of the north. I called it forth, and drew it into your service, a hardy and intrepid race of men! men who, when left by your jealousy, became prey to the artifices of your enemies and had gone nigh to have overturned the state, in the war before last. These men, in the last war were brought to combat on your side: they served with fidelity, as they fought with valour, and conquered for you in every part of the world: detested be the national reflections against them! They are unjust, groundless, illiberal, unmanly!

All the Highland regiments were raised by eminent local gentlemen using the influence of the clan system with its age-old interconnection of family and tribal loyalties to raise the requisite numbers of men. From the outset the territorial links of the regiments were vital, not just for recruiting but also for maintaining group cohesion and loyalty. The system had other benefits. Landowners who had supported the Jacobites were able to demonstrate their loyalty by raising regiments as a *quid pro quo*. They considered themselves to be Highland gentlemen and if estates had been forfeited as a result of supporting the Jacobites, the raising of a regiment was a useful means of retrieving family honour and making good lost ground. That was an important consideration, as the raising of a regiment depended on social status and financial capacity, the going rate for founding and equipping a regiment being £15,000 (an enormous sum worth £1.5 million today). As well as needing deep pockets, a landowner wishing to raise a regiment had to have contacts at the highest social level as it was the king who gave authority for the regiment to be raised in his name. Once the order and warrant had been issued the regiment came into being, and the commanding officer set about recruiting: for the senior officers a regimental colonel would look to his closest family and friends and they in turn helped to recruit the soldiers from tenants on their estates.

Regiments were also created specifically for service in India, the funds being found by the Honourable East India Company, the organisation for overseeing British commercial and political interests in the Indian sub-continent. To meet that necessity, four Highland regiments were formed in the latter part of the eighteenth century; amongst them was the 75th Highlanders, whose colonel, (later Major-General Sir) Robert Abercromby of Tullibody, was one of the best-known soldiers of the day.

75TH HIGHLANDERS

The regiment was formed in Stirling in the spring or early summer of 1787 (the exact date is uncertain) as the 75th (Highland) Regiment of Foot under the command of Colonel Abercromby of Tullibody. Amongst the recruits who joined the new regiment were men who had served previously in Highland regiments in North America, notably the recently disbanded 76th (MacDonald's) Highlanders. They were joined by 300 recruits from Perth and the surrounding Highland counties, a remarkable achievement considering that the Abercrombys had no Highland affiliations. By 1790 the first records showed that the officers and men of the 75th consisted of the following nationalities: 461 Scots, 81 English, 41 Irish and six 'foreigners'. The new colonel's military experience was a plus: Abercromby came from a family with long-standing army connections and as a young officer he had served in North America, first during the Seven Years War and secondly during the War of Independence (1775–82) where he had caught the eye of the British commander-in-chief, Lord Cornwallis. Immediately after the regiment's embodiment it was sent south to England to embark on the long voyage to India, where the southern state of Mysore was involved in a protracted series of conflicts with the East India Company.

Throughout the eighteenth century India, like North America, provided a battleground for rival French and British interests as each tried to consolidate commercial supremacy on the ruins of the Mogul empire. Although the French had lost heavily as a result of the Seven Years War – in 1757 Robert Clive's victory at Plassey had secured Bengal for Britain – the rivalries in India opened opportunities for them to support rulers who were opposed to the British presence. In 1780 British authority was confined to Bengal and the coastal strips around Madras and Bombay; the East India Company also propped up Mohammed Ali, also known as the Nawab Walajah, the ruler of the Carnatic (the hinterland of the Madras Presidency) but his authority was under constant threat from Hyder Ali, the warlike and independent-minded ruler of neighbouring Mysore. Not only had Hyder Ali proved that he possessed a sound military mind during the First Mysore War of 1767–69, when he fought against the British after he had usurped power in Mysore, but his army had been reinforced by French officers and was equipped with modern French artillery. Also, in his son Tipu Sahib he had an equally able lieutenant who emerged as a good fighting soldier during the Second Mysore War of 1780–83 and the Third Mysore War, which broke out in 1789, the year following the arrival of the 75th.

In 1790 Tipu Sultan, as he had become following his father's death, eight years earlier, invaded the province of Travancore, which was in alliance with the East India Company. A field army was created under the command of Major-General Sir William Medows, an experienced soldier whose plan was to gain possession of the province of Coimbatore before invading Mysore from the south. Coimbatore was occupied quickly and efficiently but Medows' move failed to tempt Tipu Sultan into a set-piece battle. Command of the army then passed to Abercromby's old friend Cornwallis, now governor-general of India, who had become impatient at the lack of action in southern India and the failure to deal with Tipu Sultan. Following this appointment Abercromby was promoted governor of Bombay and command of the 75th passed to Captain Robert Crauford, who later won fame as the commander of Wellington's Light Division in the Peninsular campaign (see Chapter Two). By all accounts the new commanding officer was something of a martinet and did not understand the ways of the Highlanders, many of whom, as was the custom of the day, regarded themselves as gentlemen and did not take kindly to over-enthusiastic discipline.

For most of 1790 the regiment was based at Travancore and it first saw action in December when it formed part of a force under Lieutenant-Colonel James Hartley which had been ordered to relieve the garrison at Pallyghautcherry on the Malabar coast. The operation was successful and also led to the relief of Calicut. At the beginning of 1791 Cornwallis led the main bulk of his army to engage Tipu Sultan's forces in his fortress at Seringapatam, a heavily fortified position on an island between two branches of the River Cauvery. This was reached in the middle of May but, finding it more heavily defended than expected, Cornwallis was obliged to withdraw. At the same time Abercromby led a second force, consisting of eight Bombay regiments and the 73rd (later 2nd Black Watch), 75th and 77th (later 2nd Middlesex Regiment) which was charged with the responsibility of securing the area between

Malabar and Seringapatam, a task that became meaningless following Cornwallis's withdrawal. Cornwallis made another assault on Seringapatam at the end of January 1792 using an army of 22,000 men, only 6,000 of whom were Europeans. Amongst the latter was the 75th which took part in the fighting on 22 February and lost 16 men in the process. The siege operations were halted when Tipu sued for peace and agreed to pay an indemnity to the East India Company.

The outbreak of fighting between Britain and revolutionary France in 1792 renewed Tipu's desire to achieve dominion over southern India and he capitalised on it by emerging as a perfervid supporter of the French Revolution, wearing a liberty cap and referring to himself as 'Citizen Tipu'. It was all a ruse to get French support, which was in any case readily forthcoming as the new French administration saw an opportunity to discomfit their old enemies in India. Soon French officers were turning up all over India, and so concerned were the British that the new commander-in-chief, the Marquess Wellesley (brother of Arthur, the future Duke of Wellington), decided to move against Tipu Sultan and to quash the threat before the French were able to send troops to intervene in south India.

On 20 April 1799 a force under Major-General David Baird containing the 73rd as well as the 74th (later 2nd Highland Light Infantry) and 75th Highlanders swept into Seringapatam having taken the ramparts in a matter of minutes. In the first stage of the assault a small party of stormers known as the 'forlorn hope' secured the scaling ladders and in the left attacking column these (a sergeant and 12 men) were supplied by the 75th. It was a decisive victory. Only 80 British soldiers were killed in the attack – 16 were soldiers in the 75th – but the ferocity of the fighting accounted for the lives of some 10,000 Indians, who were killed after the ramparts had been breached. Amongst the casualties was

Tipu Sultan, whose death ended the long series of wars in Mysore. Following the victory the 75th remained in India for a further eight years, and during that time the regiment was reinforced by large numbers of English soldiers from the 76th Regiment (later 2nd Duke of Wellington's Regiment). As the regimental records show, far from being disenchanted with the posting, the new soldiers quickly embraced the military ethos of a Highland regiment and in time became fervent Scots.

Throughout the following year, under the command of Lieutenant-Colonel Alexander Cumine, the regiment was employed in the campaign to control rebellious tribes in Malabar in southern India and later in Gujarat. In February 1804 the 75th moved to the Bengal presidency and, having arrived at Calcutta, the regiment was transported by boats up the Ganges to Cawnpore. Although Tipu's collapse at Seringapatam had weakened the Maratha cause it remained a potent threat, and some of the leaders caused the Company all manner of trouble. One of the most dangerous was the Maratha chieftain, Jeswant Rao Holkar, who emerged in 1804 as a daring guerrilla leader. According to General Lord Lake, the commander entrusted with extirpating Holkar, only his elimination would make the Ganges plain secure:

> I was never so plagued as I am with this devil [he wrote to the Marquess of Wellesley]: he just, nay hardly, keeps within the letter of the law, which means our army is remaining in the field at an enormous expense, and if we retire he will instantly come on to Jeypoor [Jaipur, then under British protection], where he will at least get a crore [ten million] of rupees (besides immense plunder), which will enable him to pay for his army, and become more formidable than he has yet ever been.

At the end of the year the 75th joined Lake's army and saw action at the siege of Bharatpur, where most of Holkar's forces had gathered under the protection of the local rajah. The siege proved to be a long and wearisome business, and it was not until 10 March the following year that the Rajah of Bharatpur eventually sued for terms. Once the operation was over the 75th's commanding officer, Major Archibald Campbell, issued a special regimental order praising his men for their soldierly and self-effacing conduct during the operation:

> The Commanding Officer listened with much satisfaction to the very handsome declaration of the men of the 75th Regiment, who declined receiving any payment for working when on duty in the trenches, but as that duty had been required of them oftener than expected, and as the other European corps are in the habit of being paid for it, he has also directed that it should be drawn for the men of this regiment, whose willing and regular behaviour at all times entitles them to every indulgence, and is exceedingly creditable to themselves.

In March 1807 the 75th returned to Calcutta and left by troopship for Leith. As the result of sending drafts to other regiments in India and discharging wounded men, the regiment's strength had been reduced to 44 officers and men and on its return it moved to Dunblane to begin recruiting to bring it back up to strength.

92ND HIGHLANDERS

In 1794, Alexander, 4th Duke of Gordon, raised the fourth regiment founded by his family in just under 40 years. The three earlier formations had been militia regiments known as the Gordon or Northern Fencibles and, although raised ostensibly for home service, the first of these had served in India under Robert Clive as the 89th Regiment, distinguishing itself in 1764 at the Battle of Buxar, which had been fought to quell a mutiny in the East India Company's Bengal Army. Thirty years later, when the country faced a new threat from revolutionary France, Gordon decided to raise a regular formation which would be commanded by his son the 24-year-old Marquis of Huntly. According to family tradition, two factors lay behind Gordon's military leanings. The first was his mother's desire to remove the stigma of having supported the Jacobite cause – the second duke had fought at the Battle of Sheriffmuir in 1715 and Lord Lewis Gordon, a son, had supported the 1745 rebellion. Secondly, the fourth regiment was raised by Gordon's patriotic impulse to help Britain in its hour of need in the war against France. Following a lengthy correspondence with the army's commander-in-chief, Lord Amherst, a Letter of Service was issued on 10 February 1794 by Sir George Yonge, Secretary for War, giving permission for the raising of a regiment of foot consisting of one grenadier company, one light-infantry company and eight infantry companies. To begin with it was numbered 100th (Highland) Regiment of Foot. In common with the practice of the day the Letter of Service reveals that the founder of the regiment – the Duke of Gordon – had the final say about the officers who would command it:

> His Majesty leaves to your Grace the nomination of all the officers, being such as are well affected to his Majesty, and most likely by their interest and connections to assist in raising the corps without delay; who, if they meet with his Royal approbation, may be assured they shall have commissions as soon as the regiment is completed.

Getting permission to raise a regiment was one thing; finding the necessary numbers of men proved to be quite another. The government offered a signing bounty of only five guineas per recruit (worth £490 today) and, if anything, this proved to be a disincentive for men who were loyal to Gordon but were suspicious of joining the army and did not particularly need the money. It did not help matters that another north-east landowner, Colonel Alexander Hay of Rannes, was busily recruiting for the 109th Foot which was also known as the Aberdeenshire Regiment, a title which Gordon had been urged to use himself. As a result, it did not take long for the new regiment's name to be linked to its founder and from the very outset the term 'Gordon Highlanders' was in common usage. The young marquis's absence was also a problem – he had injured his leg and was taking medical advice in Edinburgh at the very moment that his father was trying to raise the regiment. To meet the shortfall of recruits Gordon was able to raise the bounty to anything up to £20 from the income produced by the sale of officers' commissions and the regimental records provide a graphic account of the way in which every man recruited by the 100th had his price. Two recruits from the Badenoch district received £21 and one recruit in Peterhead was given £24. Altogether £2,478 12s. 5d. was paid out in bounties from the duke's exchequer at Gordon Castle in Banffshire.

The payment of the additional funds created a romantic myth around the raising of the regiment and the part played by the duke's wife Jean, Duchess of Gordon. The story appears in the first volume of the official regimental history and, while its authenticity has been disputed by many subsequent historians, it still forms a key part of the regiment's history simply because it is such a good tale:

> She [the Duchess of Gordon] rode to the country fairs in Highland bonnet and regimental jacket (it was not unusual

> in those days of military enthusiasm for ladies to wear the uniform of their husbands' or brothers' regiments). It is told how she gave a kiss to the men who enlisted – a fee more valued than the coin by which it was accompanied, as in the case of a smart young farmer at Huntly market, who took the shilling and the kiss, and then paid 'smart' [repaid the money to avoid military service while accepting the kiss], saying 'A kiss from your Grace is well worth the pound note.' Sometimes she is said to have placed a guinea between her lips. There was in a Highland village a young blacksmith remarkable for his strength and good looks. Recruiters for the Guards and Line had in vain tried to enlist him, but he could not resist her Grace! He took the kiss and the guinea; but to show it was not the gold that tempted him, he tossed the guinea among the crowd.

While it seems unlikely that the duchess would have offered a kiss to every recruit the story is so rooted in the Gordons' traditions that it would be a brave person who had the temerity to deny it in its entirety. As we have seen, a single guinea was hardly an incentive and it took a great deal more money and persuasion to find the requisite number of men. In spite of the recruitment problems the regiment was ready to be mustered by June and its original form consisted of 'one lieutenant-colonel commandant, two majors, ten captains, one captain-lieutenant, twenty-one lieutenants, eight ensigns, one adjutant, quartermaster, surgeon, assistant-surgeon, chaplain, sergeant-major, quartermaster-sergeant, forty sergeants, twenty drummers, two fifers and one thousand rank and file'. The new regiment first paraded on 24 June 1794 in Aberdeen and the next day it marched to the harbour to be transported to Southampton. Following an inspection by Lieutenant-General Sir Hector Munro of Novar, a veteran of the wars in India, the new regiment quickly demonstrated its mettle in an incident recorded in the following day's edition of the *Aberdeen Journal*:

> The men went on board in the highest spirits. The Marquis of Huntly, who may boast of one of the finest bodies of men in the service, embarked with them. He showed an alacrity of service by jumping into the first boat, and so great was the eagerness of his men to follow their noble commander, that the boat had nearly been overset; and the air resounded with cheers from those on the beach until his lordship was aboard the transport. Every man appeared to be perfectly sober, an Irish gentlemen excepted [there were 53 in the regiment], who swore by J---- that although he was half-seas over already, he would not quit the land without a quid of tobacco!

From Southampton the regiment was taken to Gibraltar, one of Britain's strategic bases in the Mediterranean, and this was to be its home until 11 June 1795, when it was sent to join the garrison on Corsica. (The island had been captured in the previous year by a small force under the command of Lieutenant-Colonel John Moore, an up-and-coming officer from Glasgow who was destined to make his name, and lose his life, in the fighting against Napoleon in Spain and Portugal.) Following a further period on Gibraltar the regiment returned to Britain in May 1798, when it was deployed to Dublin, but it was destined to be a short stay. That same year the regiment was renumbered 92nd as part of an internal reorganisation of the structure of the infantry; unofficially it was known as The Gordon Highlanders but it would be another 66 years before the title was granted by Queen Victoria. In October the following year the regiment received its baptism of fire when it was ordered to join an expeditionary force under the command of Sir Ralph

Abercromby to encourage the House of Orange to throw in its lot with the allies against revolutionary France. The initial stages of the campaign achieved early success with the speedy deployment of the allied army at Den Helder and the equally rapid capture of the Dutch fleet off Texel Island but thereafter matters did not run so smoothly. There was a lack of cooperation between the British and Russian field commanders, the Dutch were indifferent at best and hostile at worst to the arrival of their supposed liberators and there was a worrying shortage of artillery pieces. The one major battle involved a frontal attack on the French positions at Egmont-op-Zee on 2 October, when the 92nd was ordered to guard the British guns during the attack on the French lines. In the course of the fighting at Egmont-op-Zee the regiment lost 266 casualties, killed, wounded or missing, and the battle itself was inconclusive, with the French simply retiring towards the line Wyk-Kastrikum-Akersloot. Even so, the 92nd had been blooded and its behaviour attracted an enthusiastic response from the anonymous officer who recorded the battle in the *Military Journal*:

> The courage and activity of the Scotch [*sic*] Highlanders on this occasion drew the attention and excited the admiration of both sides. Those brave fellows were seen up to their middles in water struggling to outflank the troops that were opposed to them, and daring with wonderful intrepidity not only the elements, but manfully and dexterously pushing forward in the midst of a severe and galling fire.

The losses were correspondingly high: three officers and 65 men killed and 208 wounded. During the battle the regiment was under the operational command of John Moore, now a major-general commanding 4th Brigade. Their efforts and those of the supporting British regiments were hindered by the use of *tirailleurs*, skirmishing sharpshooters whose accuracy of fire and speed of movement caused high casualties amongst the advancing British redcoats. Similar troops known as *Jäger* had served in the Austrian and Prussian armies earlier in the century and had fought under British command in America, and the usefulness of these light troops encouraged the British Army to found a Corps of Riflemen in 1800.

The next contribution to the war was to be equally bloody, but unlike Egmont-op-Zee it was crowned by success. This was Sir Ralph Abercromby's expedition to engage Napoleon's army of the east in Egypt in 1801. The intention was to oust French forces from Egypt and to relieve the threat which they posed to Britain's holdings in India, but the operation was a hazardous one. Not only were the French already in position at Alexandria, but they had more artillery and possessed cavalry. They were in a good position to oppose the amphibious landings but, thanks to strict training in advance of the landings, the British force came safely ashore at Aboukir Bay on 8 March and quickly formed a beach-head, forcing the French to withdraw. The respite was only temporary and the 92nd was soon in action again four days later to repel the inevitable counter-attack at Mandora where French cavalry attacked the 92nd and the 90th Perthshire Regiment (later 2nd Cameronians). The action was described by Major-General Sir David Stewart of Garth in his history of the Highland regiments:

> On the morning of the 13th [March] the troops moved forward to the attack in three columns, the 90th or Perthshire Regiment forming the advance of the first column and the 92nd or Gordon Highlanders that of the second; the reserve marching in column, covering the movements of the first line, and running parallel with it. When the army

> had cleared the date trees the enemy quitted the heights, and with great boldness moved down on the 92nd, which by this time had formed in line. The French opened a heavy fire of cannon and musketry, which the 92nd quickly returned, firmly resisting the repeated attacks of the French line (supported as it was by a powerful artillery) and singly maintaining their ground till the line came up. At the same time the French cavalry, with the greatest impetuosity, charged down a declivity on the 90th regiment. This corps, standing with the coolest intrepidity, allowed them to approach within fifty yards, when, by a well-directed fire, they so completely broke the charge, that only a few reached the regiment, and most of them were instantly bayoneted; the rest fled off to their left, and retreated in the greatest confusion.

The main battle took place on 21 March at Canopus, between Aboukir and Alexandria, and it was a ferocious business, with the French losing at least 4,000 casualties and the British half that number, one of whom was Abercromby. Under Moore's operational direction the defending British forces showed great coolness under fire and a month later Alexandria was in their hands. To recognise their courage all the regiments involved in the expedition were granted the right to bear on their colours the figure of the Sphinx superscripted with the word 'Egypt'. As a result of the victory Egypt was saved and there followed a temporary and ultimately unsatisfactory truce with the Peace of Amiens, which was negotiated in the winter of 1802–03. Having served with distinction under Abercromby and Moore, the 92nd sailed for Malta where the regiment was greatly discommoded by the lack of tartan for kilts, which forced them to wear 'pantaloons of various sorts and colours'. On 30 January 1802 the regiment reached Cork, where the officers and men received the shocking news that the 92nd might be disbanded as part of the defence cuts following the Treaty of Amiens. As we shall see, the renewal of hostilities in Europe meant that the threat was not carried out and the regiment began recruiting in earnest, with the standard height being reduced to five feet five inches. Two years later, in June 1804, the regiment returned to Scotland en route to Colchester where it formed a brigade with two battalions of the 42nd Royal Highlanders under the command of Major-General the Hon. John Hope. Due to the threat of invasion and the worsening situation in Europe a 2nd battalion was formed in 1803 and remained in being for the duration of the coming war against Napoleonic France.

TWO

The War against Napoleon

The Treaty of Amiens proved only to be an interlude, for not only did it fail to produce a lasting peace but it was also unsuccessful in discouraging Napoleon from pursuing his territorial ambitions. Worse, the cessation of hostilities persuaded the British government to reduce the size of its armed forces: plans were put in place to halve the number of warships and to set the strength of the army at 95,000 soldiers (plus 18,000 for the Irish garrison). Amongst those earmarked for disbandment was 92nd Highlanders. Heightened tensions with France eventually postponed the economies but the fact that Britain was considering defence cutbacks encouraged Napoleon to take a bolder line in his foreign policy by planning the invasion of Britain. It was a moment of great danger but in October 1805 the enterprise was foiled by Admiral Lord Nelson's famous victory at Trafalgar and the destruction of the French and Spanish fleets. The repercussions were enormous: Napoleon had to give up all hope of invading his most powerful enemy, whom he had derided as 'a nation of shopkeepers', the Royal Navy had won command of the sea and Britain was given a fresh opportunity to pursue the war against France on the continent of Europe. Before that latter stage could be reached, though, the country had to build up an army capable of taking on and defeating France's seemingly impregnable land forces. This meant that the problem of recruitment had to be addressed, funds had to be made available to purchase equipment and the defence budget had to be increased to allow higher rates of pay.

At that crucial stage the army was helped by the emergence of two soldiers who would be critical to its development in the next ten years of the war against Napoleonic France. The first was John Moore, who had cemented his reputation as a superb field commander following his exploits at Aboukir Bay. Aged 40 in 1802, he was very much a soldier's soldier who believed in the value of training and always put the needs of his soldiers first. In common with other great military leaders, he argued that all ranks should share the privations and dangers of service in the field and he insisted that soldiers in authority should not order their men to do anything unless they were also prepared to carry out the same duty. Above all, he was committed to the regimental system, seeing unit cohesion as the best means of maintaining morale and instilling discipline. He was especially proud of his connections to the Highland regiments and to the new light-infantry regiments: on being knighted in 1804 he requested that the supporters for his coat of arms should be soldiers from the 52nd (later 2nd Oxfordshire and Buckinghamshire Light Regiment) and from the 92nd Highlanders. In his letter to the commanding officer, Lieutenant-Colonel Napier of Blackstone, requesting permission to use a soldier of the Gordons, Moore wrote in glowing terms: 'I hope the 92nd will not have any objections, as I have commanded them, and as they rendered me such a service.' Promoted lieutenant-general at the same time, Moore was responsible for organising Britain's home defences and in 1808, following an aborted expedition to Sweden (see below), he was put in command of the forces in the north of Spain, his orders being 'to co-operate with the Spanish armies in the expulsion of the French from that kingdom'.

The other soldier to influence the development of the British Army during that period was a very different personality. Arthur Wellesley, later the Duke of Wellington, had come to the fore fighting in India in the wars against the Marathas, and in the Peninsula he was to emerge as a skilful manager of men and a master tactician who had the successful commander's ability to read ground and keep one step ahead of the enemy. Unlike Moore, he kept his men at a distance and was a rigid disciplinarian who was perhaps more respected than admired by his soldiers. Known throughout his army as 'Old Nosey', he was never popular and is best remembered for his infamous comment that the soldiers under his command were 'the scum of the earth' who only enlisted for the chance to get drunk and who could only be kept in control by the threat of the lash and the gallows. There was, of course, more to Wellesley than hauteur, and no leader could have got so much out of his men if he had treated them only with contempt. While he deprecated his soldiers' depraved habits – on active service drink and violence were part and parcel of their off-duty lives – Wellesley also recognised that these same men were capable of being turned into a loyal and disciplined army:

> People talk of enlisting for their fine military feeling – all stuff – no such thing. Some of our men enlist for having got bastard children – some for minor offences – many more for drink; but you can hardly conceive such a set brought together, and it really is wonderful that we should have made them the fine fellows they are.

What kind of life did an infantry soldier experience in the war against Napoleon? In some respects little had changed since Marlborough's day. Regiments still consisted of ten companies, with eight in the centre and two slightly larger flank companies composed of grenadiers and light-infantrymen. Wherever possible the latter formations were composed of more experienced soldiers, with older veterans and newcomers in the centre. The standard weapon was still the smooth-bore flintlock rifle, whose effective range was around one hundred yards, which meant that infantry formations had to get close to the opposition before opening fire in disciplined volleys. By far the biggest change in tactics was the introduction of light-infantrymen and the use of more accurate weapons such as the Baker rifle which allowed its users to be known as 'sharp-shooters'. As used by the French, and later by the British, these new elite troops acted as skirmishers and, moving independently ahead of the main forces, they brought greater flexibility to the battlefield by opening gaps and paving the way for the deployment of heavy infantry and cavalry to exploit the initial breakthrough.

In return, conditions for the rank and file improved – but only gradually. By the end of the 1790s a private infantry soldier was paid a shilling a day, with half that amount being deducted for stoppages such as rations and laundry. In place of signing on for life, 'limited service' was also instituted to allow soldiers to serve three different periods of seven years, with discharge on half-pay in between. Marriage was permitted but most regiments did not encourage their soldiers to take wives owing to the difficulties of housing them. On home service most regiments turned a blind eye to the number of women 'on the strength' – that is, those entitled to quarters and rations – but on active service it was a different matter. An army order limited the number of wives to six per 100 soldiers and those selected (by ballot) were supposed to help as unofficial nurses and cooks, putting up with the same hardships endured by their husbands and the rest of the battalion. In 1799 the commanding officer of the 92nd Highlanders, Lieutenant-Colonel Charles Erskine, had made his feelings clear on the subject when he issued an order that his men could not marry 'unless the girl produced a good character and a fortune of at least £20'. If their husbands died or were killed, the common practice throughout the army was for the woman to marry another soldier in the regiment, usually within a day or so of being widowed.

Uniforms also changed during the Wellington years. In the 75th, which lost its Highland status shortly after it returned from India, breeches gave way to grey trousers, which meant an end to gaiters with their awkward buttons, shorter red coats replaced the traditional tailed coat and a new stove-pipe hat was introduced to offer greater protection to the wearer. Soldiers received two pairs of shoes but each shoe was the same size and shape, a practice which continued until 1847. Less importance was placed on the management of hair, which was worn shorter, and the unloved stock – a piece of stiff leather which supported the high collar – gradually disappeared. In the 92nd, soldiers wore Highland dress of belted plaid with a grey goatskin sporran with six white tassels, hose of red and white cloth with scarlet garters and a round cocked bonnet ornamented with ostrich feathers and a diced border of red, white and green. Each company had a designated hackle – white for the grenadier company, green for the light company and red tipped with white for the rifle companies. Officers and sergeants wore scarlet tunics while the men wore red tunics with yellow lapels.

75TH FOOT

No sooner had the regiment returned to Britain than it received the unpleasant information that it would no longer be considered a Highland regiment and would henceforth be an infantry regiment of the line with the new appellation 75th Foot. A memorandum from the War Office dated 7 April 1809 explained the reasoning behind the decision:

> As the population of the Highlands of Scotland is found to be insufficient to supply recruits for the whole of the Highland corps on the establishment of His Majesty's army, and as some of these corps, laying aside their distinguishing address which is objectionable to the natives of South Britain [*sic*], would in a great measure tend to facilitate the completing of their establishments, as it would be an inducement to the men of the English Militia to extend their service in greater numbers to those regiments etc.

The same measure was also applied to the 72nd (later 1st Seaforth Highlanders), 73rd (later 2nd Black Watch), 74th (later 2nd Highland Light Infantry) and 91st (later 1st Argyll and Sutherland Highlanders). At the time of the decision only one-third of the regiment's complement of 300 officers and men could claim to be Scots, let alone Highland Scots. This would be a recurring theme in the history of the Scottish regiments: a shortage of recruits leading to heavy recruitment in other parts of the country, mainly Ireland, which proved to be fertile ground for finding suitable young men ready to take the king or queen's shilling. To give an idea of the importance of Irishmen to the British Army, the 75th reached its full complement of 1,000 men within a few months of being deployed in Ireland in 1810. Although the regiment's records do not contain any figures for this period (1808–22) they cannot be very different from the other Highland regiments: of the 71st's 1,410 recruits 418 were Irish while the 74th had 1,729 recruits and of that number 716 were Irish, and 686 were English. By way of compensation for its loss of Highland status, though, the 75th had been given royal authority to assume 'in addition to any other devices or badges to which it might be entitled, and bear on its colours and appointments "the Royal Tiger" and the word "India" superscribed, as an honourable and lasting testimony of the distinguished services of that corps in India'. The regiment was also awarded the battle honours 'Mysore' and 'Seringapatam': at least its meritorious services in the sub-continent had not been forgotten.

Once back up to strength the 75th was despatched to Messina as part of the garrison of Sicily. This deployment was brought about by the flight of the king of Naples into British protection following his usurpation by Joseph Bonaparte, Napoleon's brother; if the island fell into French hands it would imperil Britain's hold on the Mediterranean and as a result the size of the garrison in Messina was increased to 8,000. At the time the British had hopes of attacking Italy in conjunction with Austria and Russia, using Sicily as a springboard, but the defeat of those allies at the hands of Napoleon put paid to that venture and by the time the 75th arrived, in October 1811, the position was in stalemate. This meant that the regiment played no significant role in the European theatre of operations in the wars against Napoleonic France. Its only experience of active service came on 14 February 1813, when it helped the Royal Navy to attack the French garrison on the Italian side of the Straits of Messina. When the conflict ended in 1815 the 75th found itself on garrison duty in the eastern Mediterranean as a result of one of the terms of the Treaty of Paris of 1815 'that the Ionian Islands should form a single free and independent state under the exclusive protection of Great Britain'. From there the regiment was stationed in Corfu and Gibraltar before returning to Britain at the end of March 1823. This was to be the 75th's home for the next seven years.

92ND HIGHLANDERS

During its period of service in Ireland and England the 1st battalion of the 92nd had come up to strength and in March 1807, while stationed at Harwich, a regimental return showed that it consisted of 892 private soldiers, 22 drummers, 50 corporals and 54 sergeants. In contrast to the 75th, of these numbers only 35 were Irish and 59 were English. The return makes interesting reading as it contains a snapshot of what kind of men soldiered in the regiment. The majority of them were five feet six inches in height with only 39 being over six feet. Only one soldier was over the age of 55, while only seven admitted to being under 18. The majority of the private soldiers (662) were in the 20 to 35 age group. Most were seasoned soldiers, with one man having over 30 years' service to his credit, while 252 soldiers, corporals and sergeants had served for between 12 and 14 years. The arrival of the 2nd battalion had proved a boon for recruitment: that May a draft of 32 soldiers arrived and the records describe them as being of 'good appearance'.

It would not be long before they were in action again as Napoleon's depredations in Europe were plunging the continent into a deeper conflict. By the summer of 1807 his army had defeated the Russians and Austrians at Austerlitz, and Vienna had fallen; the Prussians had collapsed after being defeated at Jena and Auerstadt and the Russians had sued for peace at Tilsit in the wake of a disastrous defeat at Friedland. Only Britain remained in opposition and initially its options were limited to naval operations to mount a stringent blockade of the European coastline. In order to protect the northern flank plans were then put in place for a joint naval and military attack to seize the Danish fleet before it fell into French hands. During the operation under the command of Lord Cathcart, the 92nd was brigaded with the 79th Highlanders (later Queen's Own Cameron Highlanders) and the intervention proved worthwhile when the Danes capitulated on 7 September

1807. The regiment also took part in an expedition to Sweden the following year, after King Gustavus requested allied military support. (In the event this was not required. Gustavus was of unsound mind, tried to arrest Moore and launched an invasion of Norway.) In the summer of 1808 the British force returned to Britain but none of the regiments was allowed to land as they now faced a new destination: the Iberian Peninsula.

Napoleon's response to the British action had been a counter-blockade known as the Continental System, but to complete it Napoleon had to turn his attention to Spain and Portugal. The first was subjugated by forcing the Spanish King Charles IV to abdicate and imposing military rule in the country under Napoleon's brother, Joseph. Portugal, England's oldest ally, was then invaded from Spain by an army commanded by Marshal Junot. Both were daring, if ruthless, plans but both were foiled by the refusal of the people of Spain and Portugal to accept French domination and by the British decision to send forces under the command of Arthur Wellesley to assist them in resisting the invasion. The first part of the campaign ended in farce. Following a stunning victory at Vimiero on 21 August 1808 the French army was allowed to retreat back to France in ships provided by the Royal Navy. The agreement, the Convention of Cintra, sickened Wellesley who remarked that his officers were free to 'go and shoot red-legged partridges', and it opened the way for Napoleon to assume command of military operations in the Peninsula. (The French leader was equally unhappy with the outcome as he had planned to punish Marshal Soult for his failure but as the British had obliged him by surrendering their advantage, Napoleon admitted that 'this saved me from the pain of punishing an old friend'.) At the same time a new army of 35,000 under Moore's command marched from Lisbon into northern Spain through Salamanca towards Valladolid, his aim being to link up with friendly Spanish forces. Backing for the enterprise was provided by 17,000 additional troops under the command of David Baird, now knighted and a lieutenant-general, whose forces landed in Corunna in October.

By then the 1st battalion of the 92nd had already arrived in the theatre of operations and had moved to the Lisbon area in preparation for the forthcoming campaign. As the men marched along the valley of the Tagus one of 1/92nd's young officers, Ensign Hector Innes, wrote to his parents in Cullen describing the conditions:

> We passed through some of the principal towns in Portugal. They seem at present very miserable; war is the ruin of a country. We had a great opportunity of seeing the country and the customs of the inhabitants; they put me in mind of the people of Scotland (as I have heard) twenty years ago. We have received marked attention since we arrived in this town [Portalegre]. It is a considerable place, almost on the confines of Spain, and in time of peace it has considerable commerce and manufactures. We are billeted on the natives, who are very civil, and we live like the sons of kings, but I am sorry to say not very economically; however, time passes agreeably.

The good mood continued as the battalion crossed over into Spain where their Highland dress caused a good deal of comment. Even the knowledge that Napoleon was in the field with 180,000 men did not dampen spirits. One officer in the 1/92nd simply brushed aside the information with the thought that 'It will be a dreadful conflict; we are all anxious for it and in the highest spirits.' Meanwhile Moore was being hampered by the lack of the expected Spanish reinforcements and by the news of heavy defeats at Espinosa, Burgos and Tudela. Worse followed at the beginning of December with the fall of Madrid to French forces.

The information persuaded Moore to fall back on Corunna and the 1/92nd took part in that heroic fighting retreat over the snow-covered winter mountains which left the men exhausted and at the extremes of their courage and dignity. A private journal kept by Sergeant Duncan Robertson gives a good indication of the conditions he and his men experienced during the long march north to the sea and safety:

> We were now thoroughly drenched with rain, and when night came were relieved by an equal portion of the regiment. A number of apples were found in the farmhouse, which were greedily devoured. In the evening we got our beef served out, but having neither bread nor salt, it made rather an unsavoury supper. Although the weather was cold, we slept very comfortably beside large fires we had kindled in the open air.

Soldiers prefer to forget retreats but Moore's leadership during the move back to Corunna is one of the most inspiring stories in the history of the British Army. Rearguard actions were fought at the bridges over the River Esla and at Elvina and by the year's end Moore's army had passed through the relative safety of Astorga. When Napoleon arrived in the same place on New Year's Day he realised that there would be no pitched battle, as his enemy had made good its escape. Instead of continuing the pursuit he left the rest of the operation in the hands of Ney and Soult and, having been warned of a plot against him, returned to Paris. Two weeks later Moore reached Corunna to find that the fleet had been delayed; there was now no option but to engage the French. During the fighting at Corunna the 1/92nd was posted on the left of the British line and according to the evidence of Hector Innes the regiment's pickets were soon in the heart of the action:

> The business began about half four, when the enemy rushed down instantaneously in crowds in all directions, firing smartly on the pickets (ours on the left). For a while we withstood vigorously their attacks. However, being overpowered by numbers, we retired with loss, and afterwards rallied and took post behind a hedge. I do assure you we had some fun; you would have laughed had you seen how we scampered with Jack Frenchman at our heels; but fortune favoured us. I commanded a few but trusty men, who after three hours were successful. We charged through the village along with two companies of the 14th Regiment [later The West Yorkshire Regiment], who, I am rather piqued to find, get all the merit. We certainly gave them [the French] a sound thrashing. I had the curiosity to examine the enemy's position, and was struck with astonishment to see the awful carnage; they were lying actually all above one another.

Despite the efforts of his army Moore was mortally wounded and was carried to a rear area by Guardsmen and men of the 42nd Highlanders. Like Nelson, he died hoping that he had done his duty – as indeed he had. Of the 30,000 British soldiers who marched into Corunna and engaged the French in battle, some 24,000 were eventually evacuated. Summing up the escape, Captain Seton of the 1/92nd sent a terse but telling account in one of his many letters home: 'The Battle of Corunna was bloody and bravely contested. The French got a devil of a drubbing, though five to one. As they were beat back, they always pressed forward with fresh troops. Night put an end to the action.'

The 1/92nd did not forget their dead leader. Later, the Gordons wore black buttons on their spats and black threads in their shoulder cords to commemorate Sir John Moore, a brave leader and one of the finest soldiers of his period. Also killed at Corunna was the commanding officer, Lieutenant-Colonel Alexander Napier, who was succeeded by Lieutenant-Colonel Lamont of Lamont, the chief of his clan. By the end of January 1809 the regiment was back in England, according to Innes, 'in perfect health and spirits, but in rags'. The next few months were spent in regrouping, with a draft of 220 men coming from the 2nd battalion and by the middle of July 1/92nd was ready for service again. Once more back up to strength the 1st battalion took part in the disastrous amphibious raid on French positions at Walcheren in Flanders in July 1809. Although the numerically superior British force captured Flushing the French moved their fleet to Antwerp, leaving the British forces isolated on Walcheren Island. They were not withdrawn until the beginning of December, by which time over 12,000 soldiers of the original force of 39,000 had succumbed to fever. The 1/92nd's sick-list during this period amounted to some 400 officers and men. To counteract the effects of Walcheren Fever (as it was known) the doctors recommended bathing but Major-General Sir William Erskine, who had started his career in the 1/92nd, was more forthright: his solution was a dosage of brandy on rising, another at breakfast, a third at dinner and the fourth before retiring.

It took time for the 1/92nd to overcome the effects of the fever which had cut through its ranks during the ill-starred expedition and it was not until the end of the year that the battalion was ready for service once more. The next destination was Portugal, where the 1/92nd joined a new army under Viscount Wellington (as Arthur Wellesley had become). For the next three years the British Army and its allies were to be involved in a war of movement and attrition as Wellington engaged the enemy when it was prudent and showed that he knew 'when to retreat and to dare to do so'. Throughout the campaign Wellington was uncomfortably aware that defeat would not only lead to disaster for Britain but would allow Napoleon to remove his troops for service elsewhere in Europe, where Austria had once again entered the fray. 'As this is the last army England has,' noted Wellesley, 'we must take care of it.' On 8 October 1810 1/92nd arrived in Lisbon under the command of Major Archibald MacDonald (the commanding officer, Lieutenant-Colonel John Cameron of Fassiefern arrived later, as he was grouse-shooting at Cluny in Badenoch at the time of the deployment). The previous year had seen Wellington defeat the French at Talavera, Busaco and the Lines of Torres Vedras but the 1/92nd arrived to find that there was still much fighting to be done. Most of that winter was spent within the Lines of Torres Vedras, the huge defensive system which had been constructed in two lines to defend the approaches to Lisbon.

In the spring the campaigning season reopened and the 1/92nd played a significant role in the first battle, Fuentes de Onoro, fought on 3 May. (The battle honour is styled Fuentes d'Onor.) Together with four other regiments drawn from the 1st and 3rd Divisions, it succeeded in retaking the village of Fuentes de Onoro after superior French forces had dislodged the British defensive positions. As the Highlanders went into the attack the pipe-major was shot but his life was saved by his bagpipes which, according to the regimental history, produced 'a piteous and unwarlike skirl'. Nothing daunted, the pipe-major grabbed the musket of a dying man and, having tied the bag around his neck, swore an oath to be avenged: 'We will give them a different kind of dance music!' The battle lasted another two days before the French under Marshal Massena abandoned their assault. For much of the time the 1/92nd was pinned down by heavy and accurate French fire and lost seven killed and three officers and 43 soldiers wounded.

However, for all that Fuentes de Onoro was considered inconclusive at the time, together with another victory at Albuera a few weeks later, the 1811 campaign was a turning point for the British and their Portuguese allies and paved the way for the liberation of Spain. Ahead lay the battles of Ciudad Rodrigo, Badajoz, Vittoria and Salamanca, which led to the French gradually pulling out of Spain. All were hard-pounding battles and for the 1/92nd none was so ferociously fought as the struggle at Vittoria, fought on 21 June 1813, which saw the virtual destruction of Joseph Bonaparte's army. During the attack the 71st Highland Light Infantry was ordered to climb the heights of La Pueblo to support the Spanish forces under General Morillo and came under withering fire, which cost the men the life of their commanding officer. With the support of the 50th Foot (later 2nd Queen's Own Royal West Kent Regiment) Cameron of Fassiefern was ordered by General Sir William Stewart of the 2nd Division to extricate them. The order was succinct: there was to be no retreat and the 1/92nd had to 'defend the position while you have a man remaining'.

Having reached the ridge, Cameron gave the order to advance and called to the pipers to strike up 'The Cameron's Gathering', a gesture which was remembered later with gratitude and pride by another younger officer taking part in the attack:

> During the advance a dead silence reigned through the ranks, men's thoughts being employed in the business they were engaged in. Animated by the presence of the chief [Cameron of Fassiefern], and the warlike sounds of their favourite bagpipe, the men advanced with a front as firm as the rocks of their native mountains, to meet the foe flushed with a temporary success over their fellow countrymen.

The position was duly taken and the battle was won by nightfall, but at a cost. All told, Wellington lost some 5,000 killed or wounded but the French losses, at 8,000, were greater and Joseph Bonaparte's army was forced to retreat to Pamplona, leaving behind him the bulk of his baggage train, which was eagerly sacked by the triumphant British soldiers.

The regiment then formed part of the army which marched across the Pyrenees into France and took part in the battles of Orthez and Toulouse which brought the fighting against France to an end in the first half of 1814. During this phase of the operations 1/92nd was involved in an extraordinary sequence of events which found the battalion part of a brigade of 2,500 men which faced a French force of up to 11,000 in the Pyrenean mountain pass of Maya. Despite being outnumbered they held out for nine hours and actually pushed back the opposition in an operation which forced one observer to comment: 'Never did soldiers fight better, seldom so well. The stern valour of the Ninety-Second would have graced Thermopylae.' One other action deserves to be included: the Battle of St Pierre, fought at the end of 1813, which was described by the military historian, Sir Archibald Alison, as 'one of the most bloody and hard-fought on both sides which had occurred in the whole course of the Peninsular War'. On the morning of 13 December, 1/92nd went into the attack to take the village of St Pierre and then resisted a fierce French counter-attack during which Cameron had his horse shot from beneath him. The action ruptured Soult's communications and after the battle Wellington commented that he had never before seen a field so thickly covered with dead, adding the thought that 'it was the most glorious affair he had ever seen'.

In July the 1/92nd was withdrawn to Ireland but it was not for long. Now amalgamated with 2/92nd which had supplied drafts for the 1st battalion throughout the war the regiment was back in action in Europe the following year, when Napoleon broke out of his exiled imprisonment on Elba on 26 February 1815 and set about reclaiming his position. Using the magic of his name, he rallied the veterans of his old armies and challenged the rest of Europe to respond. The result was the Waterloo campaign which led to his final defeat at the hands of the British and the Prussians, but as Wellington remarked after his final triumph over the French emperor, it had been a close-run thing. Britain and her allies had lost 16,000 casualties, the Prussians lost 7,000 and the French losses were computed at 25,000. Fought on 18 June 1815 the Battle of Waterloo put an end to Napoleon's ambitions – afterwards he was exiled on the Atlantic island of St Helena – and it is counted as one of the greatest battles ever fought by the British Army. The triumph is made more memorable by the fact that Wellington was outnumbered, his British troops had been depleted – 14,000 Peninsular veterans had been sent to America – and many of the allied German and Dutch soldiers were inexperienced. Against his enemy's advantages, Wellington enjoyed close cooperation with the Prussian commander, Field Marshal Blücher, and as a result allied intelligence about the French dispositions was more accurate.

The 92nd crossed over to Ostend on 10 May 1815 and immediately found itself amongst friends, being joined by the 3rd battalion of the 1st Foot (later The Royal Scots) and the 42nd and 79th Highlanders – 'a happier meeting could not have taken place', according to one sergeant. On arrival in Belgium the regiment was placed in the 9th Brigade under the command of Major-General Sir Denis Pack in Picton's 5th Division, the other battalions being 3/1st Foot, 42nd Highlanders and 2/44th Foot (later 1st Essex Regiment). On 16 June the brigade deployed with the rest of the army at Quatre Bras, cheered on their way by many well-wishers, amongst them a Scottish lady who was much affected by the manner of their departure:

> The 42nd and 92nd Highland Regiments marched with their bagpipes playing before them while the bright beams of the sun shone on their polished muskets and on the dark waving plumes of their bonnets. We admired their

> fine athletic forms, their firm, erect, military demeanour and undaunted mien. We felt proud that they were our countrymen.

The hamlet of Quatre Bras was strategically important because it formed the crossing of the road from Brussels to Charleroi and the road from Nivelles to Namur, and Marshal Ney had been given the task of capturing it. In the fighting which followed the arrival of the 5th Division the regiment was on the extreme right of the British line south of the Namur road and went into the attack at four o'clock on the afternoon of 16 June, demonstrating speed and aggression which discomfited the opposition and forced them to retire. In that phase of the fighting casualties in both Highland regiments were high and the 92nd suffered the grievous loss of their commanding officer, Cameron of Fassiefern, whose death in action was described by his biographer the Rev. Archibald Clerk:

> The regiment lined a ditch in front of the Namur road. The Duke of Wellington happened to be stationed among them. Colonel Cameron, on seeing the French advance, asked permission to charge them. The Duke replied, 'Have patience, and you will have plenty of work by and by.' As they took possession of the farmhouse, Cameron again asked permission to charge, which was again refused. At length, as they began to push on to the Charleroi road the Duke exclaimed, 'Now, Cameron, is your time – take care of that road.' He instantly gave spur to his horse; the regiment cleared the ditch at a bound, charged and rapidly drove back the French; but while doing so their leader was mortally wounded. A shot fired fom the upper story of the farmhouse passed through his body, and his horse, pierced by several bullets, fell dead under him. His men raised a

> wild shout, rushed madly on the fatal house, and according to all accounts, inflicted dread vengeance on its doomed occupants.

Cameron was removed from the battlefield by his soldier-servant Private Ewen McMillan but died later, having been told that the battle had been won. Like Moore, his last words expressed the hope that he had done his duty, as indeed he had. Although he was renowned as a strict disciplinarian, according to one of his officers he 'never allowed the rights or comforts of his men to be disregarded or lost sight of by anyone'. Later in the year Cameron was buried in his native Lochaber by the side of Loch Eil in Argyll and the epitaph for the monument to his memory was written by Sir Walter Scott.

Although the initial stages of the fighting at Quatre Bras had favoured the French, due in part to the failure of raw Dutch soldiers to stem the assault, the allied line held. This was mainly due to the tenacity of British infantrymen, who formed defensive squares from which they were able to maintain a high rate of fire into the attacking French cavalry. It was also won by Wellington's personal leadership, as was made evident in his direction of the 92nd Highlanders, and the British commander ended the day with the upper hand. Not only had he repelled a major French attack, but he had been able to consolidate his forces for the next phase of the fighting at Waterloo. By then the Prussians had reached the area and Wellington no longer had to fear that he would be outnumbered.

On 18 June Napoleon opened his account by attacking the allied right at Hougoumont before the whole of General D'Erlon's corps smashed into the British centre held by Picton's 5th Division. Supported by the fire of 24 cannon, 20,000 French soldiers went into the attack and a desperate fight quickly developed for the tactically important buildings at La Haie Sainte. Picton's men fired volley after volley into the approaching enemy but their position was made more secure by the successful charge of the Union Brigade (Royal Dragoons, Royal Scots Greys and Inniskilling Dragoons), who piled into the advancing French with the pipes of the 92nd playing and shouts of 'Scotland for Ever' ringing in their ears. For the Greys this meant charging through the lines of their fellow countrymen and it is possible that men of the 92nd joined in the charge by clinging on to the stirrups of the cavalry troopers as they swept past them. Later an officer in the 92nd confided that his 'Highlanders seemed half mad, and it was with the greatest difficulty the officers could preserve anything like order in the ranks'. This was one of the decisive moments in a battle which was rapidly swinging Wellington's way. Another was the defeat of the elite French Guards regiments in front of La Haie Sainte ('*La Garde recueil!*' was the horrified cry from the enemy ranks), but victory was assured when the Prussians finally reached the battlefield to shore up the ranks. That night the 92nd bivouacked amidst the carnage and mourned their dead: 82 non-commissioned officers and soldiers who were killed or died later of their wounds. Amongst them was Frederick Ziegler, a German musician.

THREE

The Long Peace, Crimea and India

Wellington's great victory at Waterloo finally put a stop to the long years of warfare with France and in the aftermath Britain was able to reduce its defence spending. At the same time the size of the army was gradually decreased and the subsequent deterioration in conditions of service had a deleterious effect on recruiting, with fewer young men prepared to look on soldiering as a suitable career. No longer needed for major campaigns against any of the great powers, the army became a colonial peace force acting in the service of Britain's growing mercantilist empire, with 75 per cent of its strength of around 100,000 men serving abroad, the majority in India. For most of the nineteenth century European affairs were generally ignored although there were occasional invasion scares and, as we shall see, a major war in the Black Sea area of operations between 1854 and 1856. Rearmament was tardy, until 1847 men still enlisted for life, a system which left the army without a strategic reserve, and, for the most part, conditions for the men left much to be desired. Barracks consisted of a wide variety of buildings from the castle at Edinburgh or the Tower of London through wooden cabins in Honduras to mud huts with thatched roofs in Jamaica. None was particularly salubrious and all were overcrowded. Bed space was limited to 23 inches in width, washing water came from standpipes, lavatory provision was a huge wooden vat and the foetid stench was made worse when soldiers covered air vents to keep out the cold wind. Barracks were also used for cooking and eating: the standard food issue per man was one pound of bread and three-quarters of a pound of meat with copper vats provided for boiling water.

It was not surprising that those conditions bred a high mortality rate. War Office medical reports in the 1830s show that deaths amongst soldiers averaged 15.3 per every 1,000 men in home stations. Overseas it was much worse in the period 1825–36: 668 per 1,000 in the Gold Coast, 130 per 1,000 in Jamaica, 69 per 1,000 in India and 22 per 1,000 in Gibraltar. Desertion was also a problem, especially in Australia and the Americas where it was easy to merge into the hinterland of a huge and relatively unpopulated country. The demography of the post-Waterloo army is also revealing: in 1830 there were 42,897 Irish non-commissioned officers and men while in the same year the figure for Scotland was 13,800. England and Wales provided a narrow majority with 44,329. As for the officers, they remained very much the same as had served Marlborough and Wellington. According to the historian Correlli Barnett, most infantry and all cavalry regiments of that period were led by men who were 'stiff-necked and haughty, rigid in social etiquette and distinctions, and dominated by a hierarchy of birth, wealth, kinship connexion and fashion'. On the credit side, Barnett concedes that most of their number 'displayed physical courage and iron self-control', important considerations when campaigning far away from home.

Such was the complexion of the army which guarded the country and its imperial possessions between 1815 and 1854, when the country was forced into an unnecessary war with a great European power.

75TH FOOT

As we have seen, the end of the war against Napoleonic France found the 75th in the Adriatic with a headquarters in Corfu and establishments throughout the Ionian Islands. This was followed by a deployment in Gibraltar which lasted two years and it was not until 1823 that the regiment finally returned to Britain. Between 1824 and 1830 the regiment's home was Ireland, where much of the time was spent on internal security duties and, as was the custom, detachments served in various parts of the country. This was one of the many unsettled periods of Irish history, with Catholic emancipation being the great issue of the day. In 1821 Daniel O'Connell, a rising barrister, formed the Catholic Association, a nationwide mass movement which called for the repeal of the Act of Union of 1800 and raised its funds by asking all members to contribute one penny a month, a modest sum which all but the very poorest could afford to pay. Although O'Connell abhorred violence and the Catholic Association took strenuous steps to keep its members in check the threat of trouble was never far away, especially in 1828 when O'Connell stood for the Clare parliamentary constituency. During the election three companies from the 75th were stationed at Clare Castle but the expected riots did not take place. Instead British observers were treated to the sight of a disciplined and well-behaved electorate who voted their hero O'Connell into power. Even the prime minister, Sir Robert Peel, was moved to comment on the 'fearful exhibition of sobered and desperate enthusiasm'.

During its stay in Ireland the 75th's movements were as follows:

1824: Dublin, Birr and Fermoy
1825: Dublin and Newry
1826: Enniskillen and Castlebar
1827: Mullingar, Clare, Limerick and Birr
1828: Birr and Mullingar
1829: Galway and Fermoy

On returning to England on 22 April 1830 the regiment was given orders to proceed to South Africa, where it soon became involved in what was known at the time as the Kaffir Wars which raged for the greater part of the mid-century. This succession of conflicts with the Xhosa people, cattle-raising tribes of Eastern Natal, came about as the result of European expansionism as Dutch settlers began moving eastwards from the Cape in the 1770s. As the Dutch attempted to create settlements this led to fighting along the Fish River and they turned to the British in Cape Province for help. Although the use of force helped to settle the issue after a fifth war was fought in 1817, the British build-up led to increased strains not only with the Xhosa but also with the Dutch. In 1834 attacks on European settlements led the British governor, Sir Benjamin D'Urban, to drive the Xhosa back over the Fish River into a new settlement known as Queen Adelaide Province, where the Dutch were offered compensation for the loss of land. However, by then the Dutch and the British were unwilling to cooperate – incoming missionaries from Britain disliked the Dutch attitudes towards the native Africans – and so began the 'Great Trek' north, which gave the Dutch the opportunity to create the new province of Natal and, in time, the Orange Free State. As we shall see, this arrangement did not solve matters but only created the problems which would lead the British and the Dutch to go to war later in the century.

Amongst the forces available to D'Urban were the 72nd Highlanders (later 1st Seaforth Highlanders) and the 75th Foot under the command of Lieutenant-Colonel England. Both regiments were involved in offensive operations against the Xhosa, receiving the battle honour 'South Africa 1835' for their role in what was described as 'continuous guerrilla warfare against the predatory tribesmen' who had been carrying off the white settlers' cattle. During the operations, in a move which mirrored the later Boer War, 50 soldiers of the 75th operated as mounted infantry. The Kaffir forces were led by a tribal chief called Macomo and never numbered more than 7,000 but they proved to be spirited fighters, many of whom possessed firearms. Eventually D'Urban entered into negotiations with Macomo and it was not until 1843 that the 75th was able to return to Britain. Their departure was delayed by the wreck of the troopship *Abercrombie Robinson* in Table Bay and the regiment was forced to return to duty on the frontier, at great inconvenience to all concerned, especially the officers who had followed custom by selling off most of their belongings before departure. Before leaving Cape Town around 200 men volunteered for service in the Cape Mounted Rifles and also in the 91st Highlanders (later 1st Argyll and Sutherland Highlanders) which had arrived to replace the 75th.

On returning to Britain the regiment was based at Plymouth and in the first few months companies were employed in a variety of activities including aid to the civil power during rioting in south Wales and providing a guard of honour for Prince Albert in Bristol for the launching of the SS *Great Britain*, the huge screw-propelled steamship designed by Isambard Kingdom Brunel. In 1845 the regiment returned to Ireland, which had been ravaged by potato blight, leading to the failure of successive crops. In turn illness struck the people, leading to increased emigration and a sharp decline in the size of the population. Naturally the appalling conditions led to outbreaks of unrest, the most serious of which took place in 1848, the year of revolution of France. Fomented by a romantically inclined nationalist group known as Young Ireland and led, albeit reluctantly, by William Smith O'Brien, a Harrow- and Cambridge-educated landowner from County Limerick, it was little more than a series of disturbances and agitations which promised much but achieved nothing. The fulcrum of the uprising was County Tipperary but it also spread into Kilkenny, and it was to Bagnalstown that the 75th was despatched by train on 31 July to aid the police in their efforts to contain the trouble. The climax came in the town of Ballingarry where barricades were put up and the police were forced to take shelter in the house of a widow called Mrs McCormack. (According to contemporary newspaper reports they sang 'The British Grenadiers' to keep up their spirits.) But that was about the extent of the action. By the time the 75th arrived in Ballingarry order had been restored and O'Brien had fled, to be captured later and transported to Tasmania. The 75th remained in Kilkenny until March 1849 when it was ordered to India, leaving a skeleton depot party of three officers. Before leaving Ireland, the regiment was strengthened by drafts from the 73rd and 79th Highlanders.

Five ships took the 75th to India and the voyage took four months, finishing at Calcutta between 8 August and 1 September. From there the regiment was transported by boat to Allahabad before marching to Ambala, south of Simla, which was to be its base until October 1856, when it moved to Rawalpindi in present-day Pakistan.

In many respects, during the nineteenth and into the twentieth centuries India was to be a second home for the British Army. Although there was a constant danger of disease – 103 men of the 75th succumbed to illness on the regiment's arrival – the Indian sub-continent was an agreeable posting for the British soldier, largely because it had the advantage of offering lower expenses and an adventurous style of life. The pace was slower too, with most of the parades and training being held earlier in the day to escape the heat of the sun. Compared with service in the United Kingdom, life in India for a soldier was 'cushy'. Even the youngest or most recently enlisted private was treated as a 'sahib', but whatever their title, British soldiers were generally excused the kinds of chores which would have been given to them at home in Britain. Cleaning up barracks was left to the sweepers, Indians did all the work in the cookhouse and the laundry was in the hands of the washer-women. In return a number of words entered the soldiers' vocabulary to be anglicised and used wherever a regiment was posted – buckshee (free, gratis), charpoy (bed), chit (written message), jeldi (hurry up), pukka (proper), tiffin (lunch or midday meal).

However, there was more to soldiering in India than the opportunity to experience an easy life – the British regiments were there to strengthen the regiments of the East India Company, which were generally led by British officers. It was in that mixed military establishment that trouble occurred in the summer of 1857, when there was a serious outbreak of violence in India involving Indian regiments of the East India Company's Bengal Army which rapidly escalated to threaten the whole fabric of British rule. On 10 May 1857 the uprising known as the Indian (or Sepoy) Mutiny began at Meerut, where the 11th and 20th Native Infantry and 3rd Cavalry regiments rose up against the local European population and started slaughtering them. The trouble had been simmering throughout the year and, amongst other grievances, the flashpoint was the decision to issue Indian troops with cartridges using the grease of pigs and cows, offending both Muslims (who regard pigs as unclean) and Hindus (for whom cows are sacred). The trouble spread to other British garrisons at Cawnpore where the garrison was slaughtered on 27 June despite promises of safe conduct, and at Lucknow where the European population was besieged in the Residency by a force of 60,000 mutineers.

When the storm broke the 75th was at Kasauli near Simla and

it was ordered to return to Ambala to form a force under the command of General the Hon. George Anson who intended to march on Delhi. (The other components were 1st and 2nd Bengal European Fusiliers and 9th Lancers, together with two batteries of horse artillery.) Unfortunately, shortage of transport delayed their departure – as part of a cost-cutting exercise the company had abolished its permanent establishment of draught animals – and it was not until 23 May that the force was able to set out. Two days later cholera broke out in the force's ranks, leaving Anson and 30 others dead. Command passed to Major-General Sir Henry Barnard and the march continued towards the Grand Trunk Road which led to Delhi. The first encounter with the mutineers came at Badli-ki-Sarai, halfway down the Grand Trunk Road between Alipore and Delhi. Here the 75th was exposed to destructive artillery fire before attacking with the bayonet to drive the opposition from their well-defended position. The regiment's adjutant, Richard Barter, later wrote an account of the engagement in his memoirs and from it the reader can see that the 'most terrible of all weapons in the hands of a British soldier' was no match for the mutineer's resolve:

> The long hoped-for time had come at last . . . and a wild shout, or rather a yell of vengeance, went up from the Line as it rushed to the charge. The Enemy followed our movements, their bayonets were also lowered and their advance was steady as they came on to meet us, but when that exultant shout went up they could not stand it, their line wavered and undulated, many began firing with their firelocks from their hips and at last we were closing in on them, the whole turned and ran for dear life followed by a shout of derisive laughter from our fellows. In three minutes from the word to charge, the 75th stood breathless but victors in the Enemy's battery.

During the short sharp battle the regiment's casualties were 22 killed and 55 wounded. Barnard had won the battle but he was now placed in the classic position of having to decide whether to press on to attack Delhi or to await the arrival of reinforcements. Although he was under intense pressure to act aggressively Barnard dithered, fearing that a *coup de main* would lead to heavy casualties in his small force. Meanwhile the mutiny was spreading into Oudh and there was no sign of the anticipated force of 4,000 which was said to be arriving imminently to reinforce him. Tied down in positions on the Delhi Ridge Barnard's force dug in and commenced siege operations and there was to be no material change in the operations until the middle of September when Brigadier John Nicholson arrived with a fresh column of troops. He also brought with him a dash and drive which had been lacking, and his appearance at the siege changed everything. Not only was he a brave and experienced soldier but he had physical presence; a contemporary description saw him as 'a man cast in a giant mould ... with massive chest and powerful limbs, and an expression ardent and commanding; with a dash of roughness'. His plan was to storm the city walls on 14 September by blowing up the Kashmir and Water Gates on the northern side of the city; leading the assault on the former position would be the 75th.

Once the wall had been breached the 75th went into the attack, 300 stormers carrying scaling ladders to the fore and with the cheers of the supporting 60th Foot (later The King's Royal Rifle Corps) ringing in their ears. At first the mutineers fell back before the assault but they quickly regrouped and poured enfilading fire into the 75th's column. At that point Nicholson fell, mortally wounded, as did the commanding officer, Lieutenant-Colonel Herbert, and realising that further action would only create unnecessary casualties the rump of the column withdrew. Brevet-Major C.E.P. Gordon then took command of the regiment and a fresh assault was made three days later. It succeeded in taking the Chandni Chouk, a main thoroughfare, but the end was now in sight. Delhi fell on 20 September and with it a major strategic position was removed from the mutineers' hands. Those who managed to escape fled from the city and made their way towards Gwalior and Oudh. As reinforcements were still arriving from Britain the regiments inside Delhi were formed into a pursuit force, amongst them the 75th and the 8th Foot (later The King's Regiment). This proved to be an unforgiving business. Mutineers were given no quarter and their positions were usually blown up – remembering the massacre of women and children at Cawnpore the British soldiers were not in a forgiving mood. As the commander of the 75th's column Lieutenant-Colonel Greathed put it, men 'forgot fatigue in chasing the rebels who ventured to hold their ground against them'.

For all that Delhi had been recaptured the mutiny was by no means over, and at the beginning of November came the unwelcome news that the Rana of Jodhpur had joined the rebellion with 15,000 men and was threatening Agra. To meet the challenge Greathed sent forward his horse artillery and cavalry (9th Lancers and Punjab Cavalry) ahead of the column, and this move decided the issue. Backed by the infantry and reinforced by the garrison from Agra, Greathed's cavalry and artillery broke and scattered the Rana's forces, killing around 1,500. Only one soldier of the 75th was killed in the action and a large number of artillery pieces and elephants fell into British hands. The next phase of the operations saw the regiment taking part in the battle which for many people back at home summed up the mutiny: the siege and relief of Lucknow in the Ganges valley. While the 75th had been engaged in the siege of Delhi, forces led by Brigadier-General Henry Havelock had forced their way into Lucknow but had quickly found that they themselves were now under siege. Lacking the necessary transport and depleted in size due to the heavy casualties the relieving force could neither escort the civilians out of Lucknow nor could it hope to engage the superior numbers of besieging mutineers. In short, the rescuers were now the besieged. To add to the problems, conditions inside Lucknow began to deteriorate, soldiers were put on half rations, their uniforms were in tatters and they were under constant fire from the opposition.

Fortunately, help was on its way. Fresh from his exploits in the Crimea, where he had commanded the Highland Brigade (see below), Colin Campbell, now knighted and promoted lieutenant-general, had been appointed commander-in-chief of the forces in India and had made the relief of Lucknow his main priority. On 12 November he arrived at the Alam Bagh outside the city with a force of around 700 cavalry and 2,700 infantry, including the 75th's column, and was able to enter the beleaguered Residency a week later. Once again, though, the relieving force was too small to hold the place and Campbell decided to withdraw his forces and establish a new defensive position at the Alam Bagh. Although the operation was a complete success – the Indian forces besieging the Residency kept up their fire long after Campbell's force had withdrawn – the feat was marred by the loss of Havelock, who succumbed to dysentery and died on 24 November. To the 75th fell the honour of forming the funeral party. The next three months were spent in creating a huge force numbering 25,664 men and consisting of four infantry divisions, one cavalry division, one artillery division and an engineer brigade. By the beginning of March Campbell was ready to attack the mutineers, whose numbers had by then swollen to an estimated 100,000; the fighting lasted 19 days and involved a good deal of close-quarter fighting before Lucknow was finally recaptured on 21 March.

Following its exertions the 75th was given a period of respite in the hills. This was a common experience in India during the hot season: to escape the heat of the plains the Europeans would move to hill stations where there was relief from the blazingly high temperatures. India was to be the regiment's home for the next four years, and in that time it was stationed at Meerut, Allahabad and Calcutta. In the aftermath of the rebellion in India steps were taken to increase the size of the garrison to ensure that the Indian army of 190,000 soldiers was balanced by the presence of 80,000 British soldiers, an arrangement which meant that between the Crimean War and the First World War most infantry regiments (apart from the foot guards) spent substantial periods in the country. For the 75th, India would always have a special place in the regiment's affections. While serving in the forces which quelled the mutiny the 75th was awarded the battle honours 'Delhi' and 'Lucknow', and three soldiers won Victoria Crosses (see Appendix). To commemorate those deeds a monument was raised in Stirling in 1863; at the same time the regiment was given permission to use the title 75th (Stirlingshire) Regiment and to wear a Kilmarnock forage cap with diced border similar to those worn by the non-kilted Scottish regiments.

92ND HIGHLANDERS

The 92nd remained in Belgium and France until the summer of 1816 when it returned to Scotland to be stationed in Edinburgh Castle, taking over from the 42nd Royal Highlanders. The regimental records reveal that at that time it was still very much a Scottish regiment; the nationalities of the officers and soldiers were as follows:

Officers: 34 Scots, four Irish, two English
Sergeants: 46 Scots
Corporals: 33 Scots, three Irish
Drummers: 11 Scots, three Irish, one English
Soldiers: 511 Scots, 53 Irish, 20 English, one 'foreigner'

A year after the 92nd returned to Scotland it was posted to Ireland, where it maintained detachments in Carrickfergus, Down, Crumlin, Ballymoney, Newton Glens, Castle Dawson, Ballycastle and Randalstown. It was destined to be a relatively short deployment. In April 1819 the regiment marched to Cork to embark on the transports *Chapman*, *Nautilus* and *Ocean*; their next destination was Jamaica, at the time generally held to be the graveyard of the British Army. The West Indies had an appalling reputation for its unhealthy climate and, as happened so often to British regiments based in the region, the main problem was illness and disease. Some idea of the problems facing regiments in the West Indies can be found in the fact that it took 11 years to repair the condemned barracks at Orange Grove in Trinidad and 20 years to build new barracks at Fort Charlotte in the Bahamas. In an attempt to address this problem the War Office introduced a regular rotation of regiments. Shorter tours of duty were ordered for the most insalubrious spots and a new pattern of service was introduced whereby regiments were posted to the Mediterranean for acclimatisation before being posted to the heat and humidity of the West Indies or North America. Later this would be extended to the eastern hemisphere, where regiments spent time in Australia or South Africa before proceeding to India or Ceylon (now Sri Lanka). Between 1839 and 1853 the British Army suffered 58,139 casualties to disease or illness and contemporary War Office papers show that the annual death rates per 1,000 men were 33 for non-commissioned officers and men and 16.7 for officers (in Jamaica it was 69 per 1,000 for officers and men).

The 92nd quickly discovered that its men were not immune to the problem and in the first six months the regiment lost ten officers and 275 soldiers to disease, mostly yellow fever. To add to the tragedy, 34 wives and 31 children also succumbed. There was a further outbreak of yellow fever in 1824 which carried away one-third of a draft of 30 recently arrived recruits. Not that it was all doom and gloom: despite the ravages of disease, for some soldiers the Caribbean was a popular posting. 'A fine country,' an old soldier was heard to say. 'Ye're aye drinkin' and aye dry.' For the most part, the regiment's duties consisted of aid to the civil power, especially on the sugar plantations where there were regular outbreaks of trouble amongst the slave workforce. Throughout its tour of duty in Jamaica the 92nd received regular drafts from the depot company which was based variously on the Isle of Wight and at Edinburgh and Glasgow. When the regiment returned to Scotland in May 1827 its strength included 37 sergeants, 11 drummers and 631 soldiers.

The following year the 92nd returned to Ireland, travelling for the first time in steamboats which took the men from Glasgow to Belfast in a matter of hours. According to the contemporary regimental records a certain slackness had crept into the men's approach to soldiering and this led to a change of command, with the appointment of Lieutenant-Colonel John MacDonald of Dalchosnie, formerly of the 91st Highlanders and a highly respected veteran of the recent wars against France. A regimental order dated 23 January 1829 makes it perfectly clear that he demanded nothing less than perfection from all the men under his command:

> The Lieutenant-Colonel regrets to perceive the books of the regiment soiled with crimes almost unknown amongst Scotsmen, viz., desertion, drunkenness on duty, insubordination and even robbery – crimes which he is determined to visit with the utmost rigour which the law will admit of. At the same time, he trusts the soldiers will not force him to such an extremity by a continuance in a line of conduct so disgraceful, but on the contrary, feel an honest pride in having it in their power to say to each

> other, 'I have never been in confinement, or brought under the Commanding Officer's notice for punishment.' And what can be a more noble boast from a soldier of some standing in the service?

MacDonald's methods appear to have worked, for within a year of his appointment the 92nd was again receiving glowing reports from the high command. He was also well capable of defending the honour of the regiment and killed a man in a duel following disparaging remarks made about the 92nd. The only misdemeanour reported to the commander-in-chief in Dublin came in an incident during a march to Fermoy in May 1832: finding that he lacked water to make the porridge a company cook took some from a supply by the door of a Catholic chapel. Only later was it found to be holy water and the priest complained to Dublin of the sacrilege done to him and his flock. Wisely, the commanding officer recognised that the action had been accidental and pre-empted the matter by awarding a minor punishment to the offender, thereby avoiding the need for a court martial. Most of the regimental duties during the deployment consisted of aid to the civil power following disturbances caused by O'Connell's campaign for Catholic emancipation (see above).

The regiment's next posting was to the Mediterranean, first Gibraltar, then Malta (1834–41) as a prelude to another deployment in the Caribbean. On this occasion the headquarters were stationed on St Vincent with detachments at St Lucia and Dominica. Once again yellow fever made an unwelcome appearance, forcing the Dominica detachment to move to Barbados. Later in the deployment there were further moves to Tobago, Grenada, San Fernando and St Joseph and the regiment returned to Britain in December 1843 after being relieved by the 71st Highland Light Infantry.

The records of this period reveal an interesting picture of the lives led by the men who enlisted in the 92nd. Each recruit received a greatcoat, red coat, white jacket and a pair of shoes but he had to pay for his knapsack, plaid and feather bonnet. Worn kilts were not discarded but the material was recycled to make trews. As for food, the fare was regular but monotonous – porridge and milk for breakfast, broth, beef and potatoes for dinner (eaten at midday) and coffee and bread in the evening. Soldiers lived in messes and were responsible for their own catering, including the purchase of extra food. In August 1846 the 92nd returned to Ireland with detachments at Belleek, Ballyshannon, Omagh, Killishandra, Cavan, Rutland and Drogheda. This was followed by the retirement of Colonel MacDonald after 18 years in command of the regiment. Later, he was knighted and promoted general; two of his sons served in the regiment and his uncle Donald commanded the 92nd at Waterloo. While in Ireland the regiment was involved in quelling disturbances during the Smith O'Brien revolt in the summer of 1848 (see above).

The Irish deployment ended in February 1851, when the 92nd was ordered to the Mediterranean station, serving on Corfu and the Ionian Islands before leaving for Gibraltar two years later. While it was based in the latter station, Britain declared war on Russia. The conflict, known as the Crimean War, had its origins in a petty squabble between the Orthodox and Catholic churches over the rights to the holy sites in Jerusalem – the actual spark was the possession of the key to the main door of the Church of the Nativity in Bethlehem – and quickly spread to become a war to prevent Russian expansionist ambitions in the Black Sea geo-strategic region. Tsar Nicholas I entertained hopes of exploiting a perceived weakness of Ottoman rule to gain influence in the Balkans, where there was a significant Slavic population, and began exerting diplomatic and military pressure on Constantinople. Matters escalated relentlessly and quickly brought the main participants to the verge of war. In the summer of 1853 Russian forces invaded the Ottoman principalities of Moldavia and Wallachia, a move which forced Turkey to declare war in October. From that point onwards a wider conflict became inevitable. Both Britain and France were opposed to Russian ambitions in the Balkans, which would threaten their own interests in the Mediterranean, and as a result they decided to shore up Ottoman rule. War became inevitable at the end of 1853, when a Turkish naval squadron was overwhelmed and destroyed by the Russian fleet at Sinope and a few weeks later the British and French fleets sailed into the Black Sea followed by the mobilisation of both countries' land forces.

The main set-piece battles – Alma, Balaklava and Inkerman – were fought in the autumn and early winter of 1854, but the regiment was denied the opportunity of taking any active role in them. As the 92nd was the most recently arrived regiment at Gibraltar it was ordered to remain there and to provide drafts for longer-serving regiments to bring them up to strength. The records show that 101 men were drafted into the 30th Foot (later 1st East Lancashire Regiment), nine were drafted into the 44th (later 1st Essex Regiment) and 124 served with the 55th (later 2nd Border Regiment). Recruits at the regimental depot were sent to the 42nd and 79th Highlanders which served in the Highland Brigade commanded by Brigadier-General Colin Campbell, who was one of the few senior officers to enhance his reputation during that ill-starred campaign.

Eventually, in August 1855, the 92nd embarked on the troopship *Orinoco* and left for 'the seat of war' (as it had been dubbed by the press) where it joined Campbell's recently expanded Highland Brigade. By then, having sent their best men in drafts to other regiments, the 92nd numbered 489, most of them raw recruits. Although the regiment's late arrival meant that it took no part in the fighting, several soldiers distinguished themselves during the war. Almost 400 served in other regiments, Captain the Hon. Walter Charteris served as aide-de-camp to Lord Lucan the commander of the Light Brigade, and Private Thomas Beach was awarded the regiment's first Victoria Cross while serving with the 55th Foot (see Appendix). A year later, in May 1856, the regiment left the Crimea and returned to its duties in Gibraltar. It was destined to be a short stay: in January 1858 the 92nd was one of the regiments sent to India to reinforce the garrison following the outbreak of the Indian Mutiny (see above). On 20 January the regiment embarked under the command of Lieutenant-Colonel A.I. Lockhart on the fortuitously named HMS *Urgent*, which took the men as far as Alexandria in Egypt. From there they went by train to Cairo before they moved to Suez, travelling on horses for the officers and donkeys for the men. The P&O steamer *Oriental* took them through the Red Sea and on to Bombay, which was reached on 6 March.

As had been the case in the Crimea, the 92nd arrived at a time when the main operations had been concluded. In the north, the sepoy rebellion in the Ganges valley had been crushed and in Central India Major-General Sir Hugh Rose, a distinguished son of the regiment, had captured Jhansi and Gwalior. All that remained was the campaign to capture Tatya Tope (Ramchandra Panduranga), one of the perpetrators of the infamous Cawnpore massacre who later supported Lakshmi Bai, the beautiful and enigmatic Rani of Jhansi, a Maratha princess who had been forced to give up her state by the East India Company. For a period of almost seven months Tatya Tope conducted a guerrilla campaign which culminated in a set-piece battle at Rajgarh. Although Tatya Tope was an inspired guerrilla leader he was no tactician and following a fierce exchange of fire the Indians retreated, leaving behind 30 artillery pieces. During the pursuit of the rebel leader, one column of the 92nd enjoyed the novel experience of riding camels, two soldiers on each beast. 'I wad rather march five-and-twenty miles than ride that muckle brute ten minutes,' was one disgruntled soldier's response to this novel form of conveyance. Otherwise, as the regimental records make clear it was a case of foot-slogging, at one point covering 62 miles in as many hours:

> During these long marches they forded several rivers, but moonlight and good roads made the men tramp along cheerily to the sound of the pipes or marching songs, though when the sun was up they welcomed the mid-day halt, dinner and grog. Latterly the road was bad, and the soldiers stumbled along, stiff, thirsty and tired.

Tatya Tope's capture in the jungles of Narwar ended the last of the rebellion in April 1859 – he was taken to Sipri and hanged for treason.

For the 92nd there was to be no return to Britain until 1863, and during that time the regiment was posted in the north at Delhi and Ambala. This was to be the 92nd's first introduction to the pleasures of serving in India, and from contemporary accounts it seems to have been an agreeable posting with the introduction of a number of sporting activities including cricket, which is not generally regarded as a Scottish sport. Daily dancing classes were instituted during the wet season, butterfly collecting became an enthusiasm and, according to a diary kept by Private Gladow, each New Year was kept in the traditional way with 'plenty of good cheer, and every one was as happy as merriment, songs of their native land and contentment could make them'. Before leaving India the regiment received a letter from the Adjutant General, dated 4 July 1861, informing the commanding officer that 'Her Majesty [Queen Victoria] has been pleased to authorise the 92nd

Regiment being designated, in addition to its numerical title, "The Gordon Highlanders", by which name it was popularly known as, and for some time after, the period of its being raised.'

FOUR

Triumph and Disaster: From Afghanistan to Majuba

The Crimean War proved to be a watershed in the history of the British Army. It encompassed bad management on a grand scale and human suffering, if not without parallel then at least minutely recorded by the watching war correspondents who were the first journalists to cover wars in faraway places. Disaster marched hand in hand with heroism, the people of the warring armies stood appalled at the suffering of the men fighting in their name and, for the first time, showed that they cared. As a result of the public uproar the War Office instituted a number of reforms to improve the lot of the British soldier and to introduce a new degree of efficiency in the way in which the army was run. A Staff College came into being at Camberley to provide further intensive training for promising officers, the Crimean conflict having exposed the weakness of reliance on regimental soldiering alone. Recruitment problems were addressed by introducing short-service enlistment, the number of years being reduced from 21 years to six years with the Colours and six in the Reserves. As for the purchase of officers' commissions, which had been much criticised during the war, the system was not abolished until 1871. The reform was welcomed but it had little effect in most infantry and cavalry regiments, where the low rates of pay and the high cost of living meant that officers continued to come from the same social background as before – mostly from the upper and professional classes and the landed gentry. On the equipment side the first breech-loading rifles were introduced in 1868 but the army's traditional red coats were not replaced by khaki until the 1880s, when campaigning in the deserts of Egypt and Sudan made ceremonial dress inappropriate for operational service. (The change to khaki was gradual and was not made official until 1902.) In appearance the regiments in the Crimea looked remarkably similar to their forebears in the Peninsula.

For the next 60 years Britain was to play no part in the wars which were fought in Europe, the main conflict being the Franco–Prussian War of 1871. Until the outbreak of the Boer War (1899–1902) which brought the century to an end, the army was to spend most of its time engaged in colonial police-keeping duties or counter-insurgency operations in various parts of Britain's imperial holdings.

75TH (STIRLINGSHIRE) REGIMENT

In February 1862 the 75th returned from India on board the troopships *Malabar*, *Salamanca* and *Dartmouth* and went into barracks at Devonport. The following year the regiment moved to Aldershot, where the first regimental canteen was established. This placed the responsibility for running the men's catering in the hands of a regimental committee which purchased all the stocks and used the profits for the regiment's benefit. By then, as a result of lessons learned in the Crimea, improvements were also being made to the sanitation within barrack buildings. Proper ventilation was introduced, piped water and decent latrines made an appearance in around half of the army's 2,996 barrack rooms and gas lighting was also introduced. The first Army Certificates of Education were another welcome innovation, with three levels which counted towards a man's promotion, and garrison libraries also came into being. Punishment, too, was changed with flogging being restricted to serious crimes committed on active service. (In 1881 it was abolished altogether.)

After spending three years on coastal defence duties the 75th moved back to Ireland in 1866 to counter the threat posed by the Irish Republican Brotherhood (IRB), also known as Fenians, who believed that Britain would never concede independence to Ireland without the use of physical force. The secret organisation had appeared the previous year and it had an influential input from expatriate Irishmen living in the United States, who provided money and weapons. As the 75th had substantial numbers of Irishmen in its ranks there could have been divided loyalties – the IRB made strenuous efforts at recruitment – but the regimental records show that only two soldiers were tempted to join the revolution. As it turned out, the IRB rebellion of 1867 was a damp squib and most of the IRB leadership was arrested. It had, however, sown a seed which would be harvested half a century later and which would lead to the later 'troubles' of the twentieth century. During the course of that same year the 75th left Ireland for a short deployment in Gibraltar, where it was issued with the new Snider rifle, the army's first breech-loading firearm. During this same period the number of companies was reduced from ten to eight, and the numbering of companies was abolished, to be replaced by an alphabetical system.

In the summer of 1868 the regiment undertook the lengthy voyage from Gibraltar to Hong Kong, leaving on 8 October and reaching the final destination on 21 December. This vital port and trading centre had been in British hands since 1842, when it was ceded by the Treaty of Nanking as an open port and in 1860 further territory had been acquired on the mainland at Kowloon. Like India it was an attractive posting, but the regiment was destined to stay there for only two years. To counter fresh tensions in British Kaffraria in the later summer of 1871 the British garrison in South Africa was increased in size. Half of the 75th was deployed to Natal, while the rest proceeded to Cape Colony. Within two years conflict had again broken out when the Xhosa leader, Langalibale, defied the government and a punitive column, including the 75th, was despatched to the Drakensberg Mountains where a brief battle was fought on 4 November 1873. The regiment remained in the area on internal security duties until it returned to Britain in January 1875, travelling on the troopships *Simoom* and *Himalaya*.

On its return, there was a further round of changes for the regiment. The Snider rifle had proved to be a stop-gap weapon and was replaced by the Martini-Henry whose heavier bullets proved to be real man-stoppers. The Kilmarnock forage cap was replaced by the Glengarry but the biggest change came in the administration of the regimental system.

For some time the army had toyed with the idea of introducing a territorial arrangement by which regiments would be linked to their own local recruiting area, and under this scheme brigade depots were created. As a result of the new system the 75th was brigaded with the 39th Foot (later 1st Dorsetshire Regiment), with its depot in Dorset, but that was only the start of the plan to create 'linked regiments'. At the time, all regiments numbered 1st to 25th had two battalions and plans were now prepared to provide all regiments with two battalions through amalgamation. Under a process begun in 1872 by the Secretary for War, Edward Cardwell, and finalised nine years later by his successor Hugh Childers, the remaining single-battalion regiments were linked with others of their kind to form new two-battalion regiments with territorial designations. Driving the Cardwell/Childers' reforms was the theory that one battalion would serve at home while the other was stationed abroad and would receive drafts and reliefs from the home-based battalion to keep it up to strength.

For both the 39th and the 75th the brigade depot arrangement had worked to their mutual convenience, with the latter supplying the former with regular drafts while the 39th was based in India, but under the revised scheme it was decided to amalgamate the 75th with the 92nd to form a new regiment to be known as The Gordon Highlanders. As the senior regiment, the 75th would become its 1st battalion and the 92nd would become the 2nd battalion. A 3rd depot battalion was formed from the Royal Aberdeenshire Militia. At the time of the amalgamation the 75th was based in Malta and the change was not altogether welcome. Not only were Scots in a minority in the regiment, but it had not worn Highland dress since 1809 and it took time for the men to adapt to the new arrangement. To ease matters, the 92nd sent a group of officers and men to Malta to show how the kilt and other accoutrements should be worn and several younger Gordons officers were posted to the new 1st battalion to increase the mix of Scots. The order to amalgamate was carried out on 1 July 1881, and when day broke an epitaph was found in Sa Maison Gardens near the Floriana Barracks in Malta, lamenting in humorous vein the end of the old order:

Epitaph on the 75th, 30th June 1881

Here lies the poor old Seventy-Fifth,
But, under God's protection,
They'll rise again in kilt and hose
A glorious resurrection!

For by the transformation power
Of Parliamentary laws,
We go to bed the Seventy-Fifth
And rise the Ninety-Twas!

The author was apparently one Sergeant Sharp and his lines proved to be remarkably prescient. As a result of the localisation changes regimental numbers were dropped and territorial names were adopted throughout the army but, as happens in every period of reform, the changes outraged older soldiers, who deplored the loss of cherished numbers and the introduction of what they held to be undignified territorial names, some of which, as in the case of the 75th, bore no relation to the new regiment's traditions and customs. From 1881 onwards the newly created regiment was dominated by the history and traditions of the 92nd (Gordon) Highlanders and although the 75th formed the 1st battalion it had to adopt, and adapt to, the uniform and trappings of its younger partner. However, the 75th's Royal Tiger survived as the collar badge and on the Regimental Colour.

92ND (GORDON) HIGHLANDERS

At the end of 1862 the Gordons made ready to return to Britain and in time-honoured fashion the men were given permission to transfer to other regiments serving in India. Some 500 soldiers took the opportunity to do this – as we have seen, India was a popular posting – but on reflection 104 took advantage of the three-day 'cooling-off' period and decided to remain with their own regiment. In January 1863 the Gordons began the four-month voyage back to Portsmouth, which took them via Cape Town and St Helena, travelling on the troopships *Middlesex* and *Surrey*. The regimental records show that the following personnel and families made the journey: two majors, three captains, 16 subalterns, five staff, 44 sergeants, 19 drummers, 448 soldiers, 23 women and 58 children. On returning to Britain the regiment was brought up to strength through a War Office order which allowed Scotsmen serving in English regiments to transfer to the Gordons in return for a bounty of one guinea (£70 in today's terms). Two months later, on 10 July, the regiment transferred to Edinburgh, travelling north on HMS *Orontes* and marching from Granton to the castle, where a soldier's journal recorded that crowds were large and enthusiastic, especially on the Esplanade 'and it was with the greatest difficulty that we, at last, got through to the gateway of the Castle'.

During the regiment's stay in Edinburgh it was involved in a number of ceremonial duties, including a review of Volunteers at Paisley and furnishing a guard for Queen Victoria during the inauguration of a statue for the Prince Consort in August 1865. (To the queen's lasting sorrow her husband Prince Albert had died four years earlier.) There were also recruiting drives conducted by the depot company and the records show that recruiting parties were sent regularly to the Western Isles, Argyll, Inverness, Glasgow, Edinburgh and the Borders. Ireland, too, remained a source of recruits but great attempts were made to keep the Scottish nature of the regiment. Good behaviour was expected of all recruits and drunkenness was frowned upon. On the regiment's arrival in Edinburgh the commanding officer, Colonel Lockhart, made that point perfectly clear when he addressed his men on parade: 'My lads,' he said, 'there are many temptations in Edinburgh and I would have you to remember that it is neither Donald nor Jock that is seen drunk in the High Street, but a Ninety-Second man.' A curiosity from this period is that moustaches were ordered to be grown by the officers and men. Permission had first been granted in 1854 but, generally speaking, only officers took advantage of the concession while the men preferred Dundreary whiskers (long side-whiskers). To keep a uniform appearance moustaches then became obligatory.

In March 1866 the regiment moved to Ireland, where it was deployed initially in Dublin and the Curragh at the time of the IRB disturbances (see above). This was followed two years later by a return to India, travelling first to Alexandria on the troopship HMS *Crocodile* and then from Suez to Bombay on the troopship HMS *Malabar*. The final destination was Jullundur in the Punjab (in modern-day Pakistan). Throughout the stay in India the regiment received regular drafts from Scotland and the monthly return for the service companies in January 1870 shows the composition of the Gordons to have been as follows:

> English: three sergeants, four drummers, three corporals, 95 soldiers
>
> Scots: 40 sergeants, 14 drummers, 35 corporals, 563 soldiers
>
> Irish: three sergeants, five drummers, 47 soldiers

There was also a change of cap badge. The original sphinx adorned with the word 'Egypt' was replaced by a stag's head with the Scots word 'Bydand' which according to the regimental historian of the period has the following meaning: 'biding, or abiding in the sense of enduring, lasting or biding their time'. In 1873 as part of the linked depot scheme the regiment was linked with the 93rd Highlanders (later 2nd Argyll and Sutherland Highlanders) in the 56th Brigade Depot at Aberdeen. In an interesting comment which helps to cast a light on later events in the twenty-first century, when the Scottish infantry regiments were amalgamated to form The Royal Regiment of Scotland, the Assistant Adjutant-General of the day, Colonel Kenneth Mackenzie, made the following observation about the need to link individual battalions into larger regiments: 'It [the regimental system] will never do, far better unite all the kilted battalions into one regiment, with one title and uniform; in time they will agree as well as the battalions of the Rifle Brigade, but two separate regiments will never answer.' A similar point was made by Colonel Duncan MacPherson of Cluny of the 42nd Royal Highlanders, who proposed the formation of a Highland Brigade which would include all five kilted regiments – 'rather than destroy the nationality of all, it would be better to join them in one regiment, with the same uniform'. As to the possible loss of cherished tartans which any change might entail General J.C. Hay, a distinguished Gordon Highlander, simply commented: 'I have worn the Gordon tartan for thirty years and I should be very sorry to change it; but I would rather have the right men in the wrong tartan than the wrong men in the right tartan.'

Throughout the 1870s the regiment was part of the cycle of military life in India – training, sporting activities and ceremonial duties which included participation in the Durbar, or 'Imperial Assemblage', in Delhi, which created Queen Victoria Empress of India in December 1876. All that came to an end in 1878 when trouble flared up again in Afghanistan. Britain had been involved in the affairs of this country since 1839, when it created a sphere of influence to counter Russian attempts to infiltrate its power towards India. As part of an aggressive policy to shore up India's north-western border the Governor-General of India, Lord Auckland, backed a coup which replaced the Amir of Kabul Dost Muhammad with a British puppet Shah Shuja, a pretender then living in India. Although the operation succeeded, the British replacement was met with icy indifference at best and open hostility at worst. It should have been the beginning of a settled rule but due to lack of funds and muddled thinking in London the British garrison withdrew from Kabul at the end of 1841. This unwise move encouraged the Afghans to oppose Shah Shuja and the British quickly lost control in Kabul. A combination of atrocious winter weather, poor planning and Afghan duplicity led to the force's complete destruction while it was making its way back to India at the beginning of 1842. Despite Afghan promises of safe conduct through the passes to Peshawar the column was attacked and the only survivor was Dr William Brydon, an army surgeon, who managed to ride into the frontier fort at Jalalabad bearing the dreadful news. British opinion was outraged by the disaster and reinforcements were rushed out to India to lend assistance to the remaining Afghan garrisons at Jalalabad and Kalat-i-Ghilzai. In fact they would not be needed, as Britain decided to abandon its Afghan policy and it was not until four decades later that there was further imperial involvement in that country's affairs.

Once again fear of Russian encroachment caused British planners to turn their attention to India's exposed north-western flank. Following the annexation of Tashkent, Samarkand and Khiva, Russia had also extended its central Asian ambitions by supporting Slav nationalists in the Balkans in their campaign to end Turkish Ottoman rule. As Turkey was considered to be the main bulwark for India's security, the British government, led by Benjamin Disraeli, feared that Russia might be making a pincer move against India and for a time war seemed imminent. (Such a move would have won favour amongst India's Sunni Muslims, who regarded the Sultan of Turkey as the hereditary khalifa, son of the Prophet, and therefore their spiritual leader.) Diplomacy prevented any outbreak of hostilities with the Congress of Berlin of July 1878, but the sabre-rattling was not stilled in Afghanistan, where the new amir, Sher Ali, a descendant of Dost Muhammad, made his intentions clear by entertaining a Russian diplomatic delegation. This caused dismay in Calcutta, where British officials decided to embark on a policy which would bring Sher Ali to heel and restore Britain's influence in the area. First, a delegation would proceed to Kabul led by General Sir Neville Chamberlain, whose reputation rests as much on his diplomatic abilities as on his invention of the game of snooker. If that failed, as fail it must for Sher Ali could not expect to survive if he surrendered to British demands, then a military force would be despatched to impose Britain's will.

In other words, the Afghan problem would be resolved by annexing the country, changing its regime and then bolstering the new leadership with money and weapons. In a later age the policy would be known as 'regime change'. Three field forces were created for the invasion: the Peshawar Field Force under the command of Lieutenant-General Sir Sam Browne (a holder of the Victoria Cross and the designer of the belt named after him), the Kandahar Field Force led by Major-General Donald Stewart and the Kurram Valley Field Force commanded by Major-General Frederick Sleigh Roberts who had been awarded the Victoria Cross during the Indian Mutiny. What followed next would enhance Roberts's reputation (in time as Rudyard Kipling's 'Bobs' he would become one of the best-loved generals in the British Army), add to the lustre of the Gordon Highlanders and create a military legend out of the example of Colour-Sergeant Hector Macdonald from Mulbuie on the Black Isle, who was commissioned in the field and went on to become one of the best-known soldiers of his day.

During the advance into Afghanistan in November 1878 Roberts's field force encountered the enemy blocking the Peiwar Kotal pass in a seemingly impregnable position. Roberts directed the 5th Gurkhas with detachments of the 72nd Highlanders in support on a night march around the left-hand side of the mountainous defile and they succeeded in outflanking and beating off the Afghans. The road to Kabul was now open. Sher Ali made good his escape – he died in February the following year, leaving the British free to enter into a new treaty which was signed at Gandamuk with his son, the new amir, Yakub Khan. While these events were taking place the Gordons were at Sitapur but shortly before Christmas the regiment was ordered to join Roberts's field force in Afghanistan, marching from Kohat to Alikhel by way of the Kurram Valley and the Peiwar Kotal pass, scene of the recent victory.

By the time spring came to the country all appeared to be quiet and to the British it seemed that their tactics had worked. Under the terms of the treaty Yakub Khan was granted a subsidy in return for accepting a new British mission led by Pierre Louis Cavignari, a diplomat whose father had served as a soldier under Napoleon. However, Cavignari misjudged the situation by failing to appreciate the strength of the anti-Western sentiments within the country and he paid for it with his life. In the middle of September news reached Simla that Cavignari and his entire embassy had been murdered. As the other field forces had retired back to India Roberts had the only available troops and he marched them rapidly to Kabul in order to carry out the orders he had received from Calcutta 'to strike terror and strike it swiftly and deeply'. (This appealed to Roberts, who wrote later in his memoirs that he would not have inserted Cavignari's embassy until 'we had instilled that awe of us into the Afghan nation which would have been the only reliable guarantee for the safety of our Mission'.) Roberts was on the point of going on leave but he quickly responded to the situation. During the operation the Gordons served under the temporary command of Major G.S. White, in the 1st Infantry Brigade, together with 67th Foot (later 2nd Royal Hampshire Regiment) and 28th Punjab Infantry.

The regiment was first in action at the Shutagardan Pass on 27 September when 100 men of C Company under the command of Captain McCallum were sent up to occupy the fort at Karatiga, overlooking the pass. While taking up position they noticed some 2,000 tribesmen moving into the pass, clearly intent on ambushing Roberts's headquarters, which was approaching the area protected only by a small force of cavalry. Colour-Sergeant Hector Macdonald was ordered to take a party of 18 Gordons and 45 men from the 3rd

Sikhs and he quickly realised that as a frontal attack was suicidal he had to remove the Afghans' advantage by moving his men higher up the defile. When the enemy did attack Macdonald ordered his men to hold their fire until the Afghan tribesmen were at close range. As Roberts noted in his despatches, 'but for their excellent services on this occasion, it might probably have been impossible to carry out the programme of our march'. The reaction within the regiment was equally enthusiastic. On Macdonald's return a voice called out: 'We'll mak' ye an officer for this day's work, sergeant!' Another echoed the sentiment by adding 'Aye, and a general too.' They turned out to be prophetic words.

It was not the end of the operations or the Gordons' involvement in them. A few days later the regiment was in action again at Charasiah outside Kabul, where the Afghans had taken up positions on the high hills overlooking a pass in the gorge known as the Sang-i-nawishta. Unable to deploy his mountain guns, Roberts ordered the gorge to be cleared by the infantry, and the task fell to Major White. With a mixed force of Highlanders (72nd and 92nd), Gurkhas and Sikhs he feinted towards the top while his right flank advanced up the ridge towards the enemy. In his history of the Highland Brigade during the Victorian period James Cromb spoke to veterans of the war in Afghanistan and wrote a description of White's leadership in the action which finally settled the issue:

> Moving his men from under cover, White saw the hills to his right lined with the enemy in many battalions. He directed the big guns to play upon the hills and then went forward with his kilted heroes. Up to this time the enemy had stood firmly against the British fire, and the Highlanders felt that to drive him from his position would require an effort of no light kind. Up they went from one steep ledge to another, clambering, toiling, but ever

> nearing the stubborn foe, and encouraged by the conduct of White, who went on with the leading files. Suddenly the Highlanders found a large number of the enemy straight in their front, outnumbering them nearly twenty to one. White's men were utterly exhausted by the climbing, and could hardly go forward, but that officer, seeing that immediate action was necessary, took a man's rifle from his hand, and advancing right towards the enemy, shot dead their leader. As the Afghans hesitated in dismay at this daring act and its fatal result, the Highlanders raised a loud shout and dashed forward, driving the Afghans down the hill, and crowning it themselves with a ringing cheer.

The action at Charasiah opened the road to Kabul which was quickly secured and 87 of Yakub Khan's followers were rapidly hanged on a makeshift gallows outside the ruined British residence in order to instil the awe of the British demanded by Roberts. The Gordons received due reward for the part they played in the taking of the Afghan capital. White was awarded the Victoria Cross and Macdonald was given a battlefield commission by Roberts, an unusual occurrence in the Victorian army and a signal honour to the man concerned. (Later, on being knighted, just as John Moore had done, Roberts chose a Gordon Highlander as one of the two supporters for his coat-of-arms.) Kabul had fallen but the *jihad*, or holy war, continued. In July the following year a British force was annihilated at Maiwand in southern Afghanistan by an Afghan army led by Ayub Khan, Yakub Khan's brother, and the news sent shockwaves through the garrison when it reached Kabul. Out of 2,476 men, 934 had been killed and 175 were wounded. Then came the news that another force, under Major-General Sir James Primrose, was besieged in Kandahar. Roberts wasted no time in drawing up a relief force of 10,000 men plus beasts of burden and camp followers which took 23 days to cover the 350 miles over trackless country in trying physical conditions. On 31 August 1880 the column reached Kandahar to find the garrison so dispirited that it lacked the will to fly the Union flag. Around the city the Afghans were positioned in the high hills and to Roberts's infantry, including the Gordons, fell the responsibility of flushing them out. These last skirmishes ended the Second Afghan War, and having put Abdul Rahman, a nephew of Sher Ali, on the throne, the British were able to withdraw once again from the country.

On 28 September 1880 the Gordons left Kandahar to begin the long march back into India and arrived at Lahore a month later. From there the regiment moved to Cawnpore, where orders were received to prepare to move back to Britain. As was customary, men could volunteer to stay on by transferring to other regiments and two sergeants, one lance-sergeant and 38 soldiers took advantage of the offer. But no sooner had the move been ordered than another order arrived informing the Gordons that they were being deployed in Natal, where they were needed to reinforce an army being assembled for service in the Transvaal.

War with the resident Boer (Dutch immigrant) population had become inevitable in 1881, when they refused to pay taxes and declared independence. The conflict, which became known as the First Boer War, was a bad business for Britain with undignified defeats at Bronkhorstpruit, Ingogo River and Laing's Nek, and the British public was treated to the spectacle of well-trained British soldiers being defeated by what seemed to be an army of peasant farmers. On one level the public had good reason for concern: the Boers were mobile, expert marksmen and they knew the lie of the land. However, their strengths also contained some weaknesses: if camouflage and precision were their strong points they were often lacking in discipline, many Boers not thinking twice before drifting off home following an engagement. That being said, through their military abilities the Boers gained a reputation for invincibility which was to stand them in good stead both during this war and its successor, which broke out in 1899.

For the Gordons the fighting against the Boers was dominated by an action at Majuba Hill which was to be remembered both for the wrong-headedness which sent the regiment into action and for the tenacious courage of those caught up in the fighting. On arriving at Durban at the end of January the Gordons came under the command of Major-General Sir George Colley. A brilliant man, almost renaissance in his ability to embrace interests as diverse as political economy, painting and poetry, Colley's Achilles heel was his inability to accustom himself to the rough and tumble of campaigning. He was also introspective and indecisive and, fatally for those under his command, he underestimated the Boers' skills as mounted infantrymen. Almost everything he attempted went wrong and it was perhaps inevitable that he would make the blunders that led to the defeat at Majuba. The main problem was that Colley was unsure what to do to initiate operations against the Boers. Having established a forward base in the Drakensberg Mountains, he was ordered by London to inform the Boer leadership that if they stopped their rebellion talks would be held to address their grievances and hostilities would be suspended for 48 hours. At the same time Colley was uncomfortably aware that the Boers were reinforcing a position in a narrow defile known as Laing's Nek. Colley believed that it was possible to retrieve the initiative without breaking the truce, but this would entail scaling the heights of the 6,500 ft-high Majuba Hill, an extinct volcano which towered above the Natal border and which overlooked the Boer position at Laing's Nek.

To capture the hill Colley selected a small force made up from the following regiments and placed under his personal command:

Three companies, 92nd Highlanders (Major Hay and 180 rifles)
Two companies 3/60th (Captain Smith and 140 rifles)
Two companies 58th (Captain Morris and 170 rifles)
Naval Brigade (Commander Romilly and 64 rifles)

The two other infantry regiments in the attack, the 58th and the 3/60th, later became, respectively, 1st Northamptonshire Regiment and The King's Royal Rifle Corps. The march up the precipitous slopes was made in the darkness of the night of 26 February and was made doubly difficult by the kit carried by each man: rations for six days, water, a blanket and greatcoat, waterproof shelter and 70 rounds of ammunition. 'It was a fearful climb,' wrote Lieutenant (later Lieutenant-Colonel) Forbes Macbean of the Gordons, who took part in the attack, 'and it is a perfect mystery to me how men with pouches full of ammunition, carrying rolled blankets and greatcoat, could ever have got up in daylight, much less on a pitch-dark night'. When they eventually reached the summit the exhausted soldiers discovered a saucer-shaped plateau which gave them superb views over the surrounding countryside, including the Boer position below, but already their own position was in jeopardy. Instead of entrenching the summit the men relaxed, with the Gordons holding the ridge overlooking the Boer camp. That lack of activity was to prove a fatal error. At dawn the Boers noted the British presence on Majuba and prepared to storm the heights, making their way by pony up the northern flank before attacking the British position. At first most of their shots went high but the lack of entrenchment soon told as the Boers poured volley after volley into the British ranks, creating panic amongst those attempting to hold the hill. One of the Gordons subalterns, Lieutenant (later General Sir) Ian Hamilton, asked Colley for permission to charge with the bayonet but the answer came back: 'Not yet, wait until they cross the open, and then we will give them a volley and a charge.'

That moment never came and all the while the Boers used their hidden position to fire at will into the British ranks. By early afternoon the superior firepower began to tell and the depleted British force began to retire to the safety of the lower ground. Of the 180 officers and men of the Gordons who climbed Majuba 44 were killed or died as a result of their wounds and 52 were wounded. It was hardly a rout and none of the soldiers was found dead with a bullet in his back, but it was a bleak day for national pride. Colley himself was killed as was the commander of the Naval Brigade and almost 75 per cent of the British force became casualties. Coming on top of the regiment's highly publicised success in Afghanistan Majuba was a black day for the Gordons, but amidst the panic and the confusion there were men who behaved with courage and dignity. In the papers of Major G.S. White and Major J.C. Hay it is clear that confusion and muddle reigned for much of the fighting and that the men of the Gordons were not to blame for the disaster. Ian Hamilton rallied his men until shot through the wrist and, bleeding heavily, would have been killed by a young Boer but for the intervention of an older man who pushed the youngster aside. In his after-battle report written on 9 March Major-General Sir Evelyn Wood made special mention of Private John Murray and recommended him for the award of a Distinguished Service Medal:

> Private John Murray was close to the brow over our line of advance during the final forward movement of the Boers. A Scotsman in the Boer ranks called upon Private Murray to surrender. The latter replied, 'I'll see you d----d first,' and jumped down, receiving a bullet in the arm. Halfway down the hill his knee fell out of joint but, obtaining the assistance of a comrade to restore it to place, he returned

> at six o'clock with his rifle and side-arms to camp, where he was seen by Second-Lieutenant Sinclair Wemyss, 92nd Highlanders.

The same despatch also noted 'the conspicuous gallantry' displayed by others, including Second-Lieutenant Hector Macdonald, who was taken prisoner and would have had his sword removed from him but for the intervention of the Boer leader Pieter Joubert. It was a dignified end to what had been a miserable affair. All the British prisoners were well treated during their short time in captivity and the Boers had the last word when Hamilton said in exasperation that, 'This was a bad day for us.' Back came the reply from Joubert: 'What can you expect from fighting on a Sunday?'

Following the action the Gordons remained in the Drakensberg area and on 30 June came the news of the amalgamation with the 75th. The occasion was marked by a mock funeral in which a coffin containing a flag inscribed '92' was carried in a torchlit procession to the grave. Three rifle volleys were fired over it and the pipers played a lament. It was not the end of the business: next morning the 2nd battalion (as it had become) woke to find that the 'grave' had been exhumed and that on the flag, alongside the numerals, was the defiant message: 'No' deid yet.' In November the battalion returned to Durban prior to the voyage back to Britain on board the troopship *Calabria*. At the time of the amalgamation the composition of the new regiment's three battalions was as follows:

> 1st battalion: 28 officers, two warrant officers, 48 sergeants, 44 corporals, 21 drummers and pipers, 760 soldiers. Total 903.
>
> 2nd battalion: 24 officers, two warrant officers, 40 sergeants, 40 corporals, 21 drummers and pipers, 480 soldiers. Total 607.

THE GORDON HIGHLANDERS

3rd depot battalion: five officers, one warrant officer, ten sergeants, ten corporals, two drummers and pipers, 40 soldiers. Total 68.

FIVE

The Gay and Gallant Gordons

For the first years of the regiment's new life the 1st battalion was the overseas battalion, while the 2nd battalion formed the home service battalion, sending regular drafts and reliefs to the former. Although the system had been broadly welcomed, it was still not altogether efficient. Throughout the remainder of the century home-based battalions experienced immense problems in finding the necessary numbers of men and were often so depleted that they had difficulty keeping up to strength themselves. All too often they had to enlist volunteers from other regiments or had to call on reservists. Due to the slow pace of reform pay remained low and conditions continued to be antiquated, and as a result recruiting targets were rarely met. Marriage was still discouraged, drunkenness was rife and those who left the army often became unemployed vagrants or burdens on society. With the decline of the rural population a traditional source of recruitment was drying up; this was a particular problem for regiments like the Gordons, whose recruitment hinterland was largely made up of country areas. Despite the abolition of purchasing commissions the social background of the army's officers did not change and Britain's military officer class still came from the aristocracy, the landed gentry, the clergy and the professions and had been educated at Britain's great private schools.

There were, of course, a number of successful innovations. The earlier introduction of the new breech-loading rifles had helped to increase the rate and weight of fire and this was assisted by the use of new smokeless propellants. The Royal Artillery started receiving breech-loading ordnance and in the Maxim gun the army possessed a reliable automatic machine-gun which gave it astonishing firepower. In Garnet Wolseley the army also possessed one of the great military reformers. One of the rising stars in the British Army, Wolseley had served in the Crimea and in India during the mutiny and as he climbed up the army lists he made a point of personally selecting his officers and nurturing military talent. In time, the officers who served with him would be known as the 'Wolseley Ring' and once they had come to his notice their careers usually prospered. (One exception was Colley, whose career ended in ignominy at Majuba Hill.) A rival 'ring' was formed by Roberts in India but Wolseley's was the more influential of the two. In 1869 he had published *The Soldier's Pocket Book*, which became the standard military textbook of its day with its insistence on the need for thorough and painstaking preparation before undertaking any operation. Wolseley was also an experienced soldier: having served as a subaltern in Burma, China, India and the Crimea he had gone on to make his name as an operational commander in Canada (Red River Expedition, 1870) and the Ashanti War of 1873–74. Not for nothing was the phrase 'All Sir Garnet' a byword for efficiency and good practice. In 1895 he became commander-in-chief of the British Army, succeeding his great rival, the deeply conservative Duke of Cambridge, who was Queen Victoria's cousin.

One thing neither Wolseley nor his army was ever denied – the chance to see operational service. Between 1883 and 1914 not a year passed without British soldiers being in action in one part of the empire or the other. Although the operations were usually policing actions against unequal native opposition, they allowed the new weapons to be tested and, above all, they made soldiers familiar with battlefield conditions. Drawing from his own career, Wolseley argued that experiences of this kind were absolutely essential, especially 'the sensation of being under fire'. It helped too that the opposition was varied – tribal warriors with primitive weaponry but unlimited courage (Maoris, Ashanti, Zulus), hillmen with an intimate knowledge of the lie of the land (Afghans and Pathans), fundamentalists with no fear of death (Dervishes and Mahdists), well-organised infantry (Egyptians) and equally skilful mounted infantry (Boers). All those operations brought different challenges to the soldiers who experienced them and helped to fashion the late Victorian and Edwardian soldier in the three decades before the outbreak of the First World War.

1ST BATTALION

No sooner had 1st Gordons come into being than the battalion was offered the opportunity of being tested in battle. At the beginning of August 1882 the battalion left Malta for Alexandria in Egypt, to join the Highland Brigade under the command of Major-General Archibald Alison as part of a force sent to protect British interests in the country. (The other battalions in the brigade were 2nd Highland Light Infantry, 1st Black Watch and 1st Cameron Highlanders.) Britain had a vested interest in controlling Egypt's internal affairs following the opening of the Suez Canal in 1869 and the purchase of shares in the operating company six years later. Obviously, this state of affairs created local tensions and the 1880s began with an upsurge of nationalist demonstrations aimed against the British presence. As the situation deteriorated Britain decided to intervene to restore order after the Egyptian army, led by Colonel Ahmed Arabi, began a rebellion to regain control of the country. Wolseley was given command of the force, which numbered 40,500, at that time the largest expeditionary force put together by the British Army.

Ahead of his landing Wolseley let it be known that he intended to make landfall at Aboukir Bay before moving on Alexandria but that was only a ruse. His real destination was Port Said, where he landed his forces on 1 September and at Ismailia took possession of the Suez Canal. From there Wolseley's army moved west, defeating an Egyptian force at Tel-el-Mahuta before concentrating at Kassassin for the assault on the main Egyptian base at Tel-el-Kebir. Arabi thought that his position was impregnable and that the British would be unable to withstand the fierce midday heat to make their expected assault. But having inspected the position Wolseley decided to take part of his force across the desert by night on 12 September, with the Highland Brigade in the vanguard. Naval officers accompanied the infantry columns to navigate by the stars and before sunlight the following day the force was in sight of the Egyptian defensive positions. The Highland Brigade then went into the attack with 1st Gordons and 1st Camerons in the centre and 1st Black Watch on the right flank. Their target was formed of high parapets and deep ditches, where the Egyptian soldiers were taken by surprise and stood little chance in the face of the speed and strength of the Highlanders' charge. Inside the defences there was fierce hand-to-hand fighting which left around 2,000 Egyptian soldiers dead in just under two hours. In his history of the Highland Brigade James Cromb quotes at length from Alison's recollections of the action in which 1st Gordons played a conspicuous role:

> On the right of the Brigade the advance of the Black Watch was arrested, in order to detach some companies against a strong redoubt, the artillery from which was now in the breaking light playing heavily on General Graham's brigade and our own advancing guns. So earnest were the Egyptian gunners here that they were actually bayoneted after the redoubt had been entered from the rear whilst still working their pieces. Thus it came about that, from both the flank battalions of the brigade being delayed, the charge straight to their front of the Gordon and Cameron Highlanders in the centre caused these to become the apex of a wedge thrust into the enemy's line . . . At this point it was a noble sight to see the Gordon and Cameron Highlanders, now mingled together in the confusion of the fight, their young officers leading with waving swords, their pipes screaming, and that proud smile on the lips and bright gleam in the eyes of the men which you see only in the hour of successful battle. At length the summit of the gentle slope we were ascending was reached and we looked down upon the camp of Arabi lying defenceless below us.

During the action the 1st battalion's casualties were two officers and six soldiers killed and one officer and 29 soldiers wounded. The victory at Tel-el-Kebir ended Arabi's revolt and Wolseley was able to send a telegraph to the War Office telling them not to send any more troops to Egypt. However, there was no respite for the 1st battalion, which went on to help capture the important railway junction at Zagazig and was present at the surrender of the Egyptian garrison at Salahieh.

Following the crushing of the rebellion Arabi and his main lieutenants were spared the death penalty but were sent into exile on the island of Ceylon (now Sri Lanka). An army of occupation remained in Egypt to prevent any further outbreaks of trouble and amongst its ranks was 1st Gordons under the command of Lieutenant-Colonel D. Hammill. Little did the Gordons know it, but this was just the beginning of their adventures in the region. Two years later the battalion was in action again when it formed part of a force under the command of Major-General Sir Gerald Graham which was sent into neighbouring Sudan to deal with an Islamic fundamentalist revolt led by Mohammed Ibn Al-Sayd Abdullah, a self-styled descendant of the prophet Mohammed (Mahdi or 'expected one'), who intended to rid Sudan of infidel forces. As news began to filter out of the fall of local Egyptian garrisons and the slaughter of those opposed to Mahdist ideals, Britain decided to act by sending a punitive expedition into the area. The force was taken by convoy to the port of Suakin, the last remaining town held by the Egyptian forces in Sudan, which was being threatened by dervish forces (the name given to the Mahdi's soldiers) under the command of Osman Digna, a ruthless Turkish-Sudanese slave-dealer.

From Suakin Graham struck inland and on 29 February 1884 annihilated a Mahdist force at El Teb, where an Egyptian force had been cut to pieces the previous year. Over 2,000 dervishes were killed by the superior firepower of the British Gatling guns. During the action half of 1st Gordons was called on to reinforce the square (then the army's main defensive formation) after it became 'irregular' while the other half continued to protect the flanks. Two weeks later there was another battle at Tamai, where Osman Digna personally commanded the Mahdist army and almost inflicted a defeat on Graham's force. During the advance the 2nd Brigade's square almost broke in the confusion of the dervish attack. With the square ruptured in one place the defenders could not open fire on those who rushed into the breach without taking the risk of firing on their own soldiers. It was a desperate situation but discipline was soon restored. By the beginning of April the force, including 1st Gordons, was back in Cairo where, according to the regimental historian, 'the Camerons, with true Highland hospitality, had provided entertainment for their friends'.

While these events were unfolding General Charles Gordon, a Royal Engineer and one of the most charismatic soldiers in the British Army, was in Khartoum attempting to evacuate it before it fell into the hands of Mahdist forces. The tragedy of his story is soon told. On 18 February 1884 he entered the city, where his arrival was met with acclaim, but even as he attempted to make sense of the situation Khartoum was surrounded by 3,000 dervishes under the command of the Mahdi. At home in Britain there was a public outcry to save Gordon before it was too late and Wolseley was given command of the relief force. He faced an enormous challenge, as the Mahdists had cut off the Nile route and the hinterland of Suakin was also in their control. To overcome that difficulty he produced a plan which involved his army following the course of the Nile in November until it reached Korti, where the great river makes a bend eastwards. There, a Desert Column composed of 1,100 men under the command of Major-General Sir Herbert Stewart would strike off across the Bayuda Desert to Metemma above Khartoum and attempt to make contact with Gordon. At the same time a River Column including 1st Gordons would continue the journey up the Nile towards Berber. For both columns it proved to be a wretched business. Stewart's men had to contend with the fierce heat and unyielding terrain of the Bayuda Desert while the River Column had to manhandle their big whaling boats up the difficult waters of the Nile with its many cataracts.

Their suffering was all in vain. On 28 January 1885 a small advance party from the River Column got within sight of Khartoum to find unmistakable evidence that the city had fallen into Mahdist hands. Buildings were ruined and the Union flag no longer flew from the palace roof, a sure sign that Gordon was dead. In fact, the Mahdists had entered Khartoum two days earlier and in the midst of the ensuing violence Gordon had been dragged out and killed. There was nothing for the advance party to do but turn around and return to Metemma. By then the River Column, including 1st Gordons, had advanced as far as Kirbekan, where D Company under Hamilton's command was involved in a hot engagement with the dervishes, but with Gordon's death there was no point in continuing the expedition and on 24 February Wolseley gave the order to begin the long retreat back into Egypt. The Gordon Relief Expedition, as it became known, returned to Cairo in September 1885. It received the thanks of both houses of parliament, Wolseley was created a viscount and there were medals for all the soldiers involved but the fact remained that Britain had been forced out of Sudan and it would take another 14 years before Gordon's death was avenged. The battalion then returned to Malta, which was to be its base until November 1888 when it transferred to Ceylon, taking with it a complement of 25 officers, two warrant officers, 47 sergeants, 40 corporals, 21 drummers and 760 soldiers. Some idea of the life led by the battalion on the island can be found in the regimental records, as related by Lieutenant-Colonel Greenhill Gardyne:

> Officers and men enjoyed their visit to this lovely island. At Colombo there were many Scots among the tradesmen of the town, who exchanged hospitalities with the members of the sergeants' mess; matches at cricket and football were played with the planters from the interior; the officers played polo, and all ranks made excursions along the palm-shaded roads, and bathed in the breakers on the beach at Mount Lavinia. Kandy, one of the most beautiful spots in creation, and much frequented by tourists, was a pleasant

> quarter, cooler than Colombo, and within reach by rail of Newera Eliya, famous for its climate and tea-gardens. From Trincomalee the men made excursions in the neighbouring forests as far as Kantalai, shooting wild pig, deer and jungle fowl, while officers penetrated still further into the wonderful jungles, camping out and enjoying a sport which is itself the best military training, and which included every sort of game from a snipe to an elephant.

The idyll ended at the beginning of 1893, when 1st Gordons left Colombo and sailed for Karachi before moving north into the Punjab, where the battalion was based first at Ambala and then at Rawalpindi. In October 1894 the battalion marched 170 miles to take part in a Viceregal Durbar at Lahore, which the regimental historian describes as being 'gay with the picturesque retinues of native grandees, who, in gorgeous garments of silk and satin – light green, saffron or orange, wonderfully embroidered coats, and often, especially the frontier folk, immense parti-coloured turbans – gave brilliancy to the scene'. No sooner had the battalion participated in the celebrations than it was ordered once more on active service.

This time it was to be new territory for the battalion – the North-West Frontier Province, home of some of the most mettlesome tribes in British India. The trouble flared in Chitral, where the British Political Agent was besieged together with the remains of his garrison following a local disturbance involving rival families. A relief force was put together under the command of Major-General Sir R.C. Low and 1st Gordons served in the 2nd Brigade under Brigadier-General H.G. Waterfield. In wet and cold weather conditions the force set out for the Malakand Pass, where the Gordons went into the attack with 2nd King's Own Scottish Borderers, prompting the soldier and explorer Sir George Younghusband to write in his account of the expedition: 'It was a fine and stirring sight to see the splendid dash with which the two Scottish regiments took the hill.' Having taken the pass Low's force pushed on Chitral, which was eventually relieved on 2 April 1895. It was not until mid-September that the battalion was able to return to its base at Rawalpindi. Two years later, in August 1897, 1st Gordons was part of another punitive expedition, the Tirah Expeditionary Force under the command of Major-General Sir William Lockhart which was formed to put down a rebellion by the Afridi and Orakzai tribes which had been attacking British positions along the frontier.

In this new operation the Gordons were brigaded with 1st Dorsets, 1/2nd Gurkha Rifles and 15th Sikhs under the command of Ian Hamilton, now a brigadier-general. The battalion's moment came on 20 October when it was ordered to attack an enemy position on the Dargai Heights. Situated on a rocky spur at the head of the Chagru Valley it had defied efforts to storm it two days earlier, but it had to be captured as it dominated the road through which Lockhart's forces had to pass. The task of storming the position was given to 1st Gordons (see Chapter One for the words of the order) and at 2.00 p.m. the battalion moved forward through positions held by the Dorsets and, pipes playing, went into the attack. Lockhart's post-battle despatch provided a vivid description of what happened next:

> It [1st Gordons] dashed through a murderous fire, and in forty minutes had won the heights, leaving three officers and thirty men killed or wounded on its way. The first rush of the Gordons was deserving of the highest praise, for they had just undergone a very severe climb, and had reached a point beyond which other troops had been unable to advance for over three hours. The first rush was followed at short intervals by a second and a third, each led by officers,

> and as the leading companies went up the path for the final assault, the remainder of the troops, among whom 3rd Sikhs were conspicuous, streamed on in support. But few of the enemy waited for the bayonet, many of them being shot down as they fled in confusion.

As Lockhart made clear, other regiments, English and Indian, also took part in the attack on Dargai but it was the Gordons who got all the glory. Mainly this was due to the élan and courage shown by the men in the final phase of the attack, but it was also helped by the courage shown by Piper George Findlater, who continued to play his pipes despite being wounded in both legs. In time it would become one of the celebrated images of the age – Highlanders going into the attack spurred on by the pipes. Later, on his return to Britain, Findlater was fêted as a hero and, according to the regimental historian, 'the Scotsmen in London would have let him swim in champagne' but that fame was bought at a cost. He was tempted to take part in re-enactments of the attack and these performances led to considerable ill-feeling within the regiment. Later, Findlater rejoined the Gordons for home service on the outbreak of the First World War, and died in 1942 having taken up farming in Banffshire.

It was not the end of the campaign, but the storming of the heights at Dargai had dented Afridi confidence and for the next year Lockhart used his forces on a number of punitive expeditions to show the hillmen that their territory was not impregnable. In April 1898 the battalion returned to India, where it was stationed at Gharial in the Murree Hills, a cool-weather station. While stationed there, orders arrived to prepare to return to Britain with 514 non-commissioned officers and men staying behind to join the 2nd battalion, which was on its way out to India. By a happy coincidence, when 1st Gordons prepared to leave India for Britain in October 1898 it met the 2nd battalion at Bombay's transit camp at Deolali just as it was about to deploy in India. (The name of the barracks gave rise to the soldier's slang word 'doolally' which was applied to men whose nerves had cracked and were waiting to be transported home.) Little did either battalion realise it at the time, but they would soon be serving together again when war broke out in South Africa.

This proved to be a costly and humiliating conflict not just for the British Army but also, as it turned out, for the Scottish regiments involved. For most of the nineteenth century Britain had been at loggerheads with the Boers. The migration of the Dutch to Transvaal and the Orange Free State had not improved matters and, as we have seen, the enmity had erupted into open war in 1880. Following the humiliating defeat at Majuba Hill an uneasy peace had been restored, with the Boers operating self-government under British suzerainty, but it was only a stop-gap arrangement. In 1886 seemingly limitless supplies of gold were discovered in Boer territory south of Pretoria and the promise of untold riches attracted speculators from Britain and all over Europe. Before long the Boers were outnumbered by outsiders who threatened their traditional, conservative way of life. To protect the interests of his fellow Boers in the Transvaal President Kruger passed stringent laws excluding non-Boers from participation in political life while retaining the right to tax them.

Such a state of affairs was bound to cause irritation, but the British response in 1895 only caused further trouble. Acting in the mistaken belief that an uprising against the Boers was imminent the British imperial adventurer Cecil Rhodes encouraged his associate Dr Starr Jameson to lead a raid into the Transvaal to bring down Kruger's government. The so-called 'Jameson Raid' was a fiasco, Rhodes was disgraced, Britain was made a laughing stock and to make matters worse the subsequent negotiations to retrieve the situation settled nothing. Each new concession was met with further demands and gradually war became inevitable. In 1899 Britain despatched 10,000 troops to South Africa to bolster its garrison while the Transvaal, now backed by the Orange Free State, made plans for mobilisation. Within a week of the declaration of war General Sir Redvers Buller VC was on his way to South Africa to take command of the imperial forces in what everyone hoped would be a short, sharp war. Amongst those regiments heading south was 1st Gordons, which was mobilised for service on 2 October travelling from Edinburgh by train to Liverpool, and then onwards to Cape Town on board the Bibby liner *Cheshire*. Its final destination was the Orange River, some 20 miles from Kimberley.

The battalion arrived in time to play a part in the disastrous Battle of Magersfontein involving the Highland Brigade, which had been ordered to engage a prominent Boer position as part of a general advance to raise the siege of Kimberley. From the very outset the operation was doomed. Reconnaissance of the Boer position was sketchy, the Highland Brigade had to make a night march through torrential rain to get into position for a dawn attack and the artillery bombardment failed to cause any damage as the Boers had moved their defensive lines. When the Highland Brigade went into the attack the Scottish battalions came under sustained and accurate rifle fire from the hidden Boers and casualties mounted. Very quickly the brigade was pinned down by sniper fire; without food or water and tormented by the scorching sun, the Highlanders' nerve broke and they began a panic-stricken retreat to safety. The news of the disaster caused a tremendous shock when it reached Scotland and the misery was compounded by news of two other heavy defeats at Stormberg and Colenso, a period of setbacks that the war correspondent Arthur Conan Doyle christened 'Black Week'.

Methuen then used 1st Gordons and 1st Scots Guards to stabilise the position, and during the subsequent fighting the Gordons lost their commanding officer Lieutenant-Colonel G.S. Downman. All told, the Gordons lost two other officers killed, two wounded and six soldiers killed and 19 wounded. As seen in the writing of Lieutenant-Colonel Forbes Macbean who succeeded Downman, Magersfontein was a tragedy, pure and simple: 'Thus ended an unsatisfactory action that commenced with disaster. The force remained for nine hours under the close fire, and in full view, of the enemy; in terrific heat, with no water but one's own bottle, with no target; worst of all, with no orders of any description.'

Following the battle 1st Gordons moved to Enslin, where 107 of their number left the battalion to join the 6th Mounted Infantry. These units had been ordered by the War Office as 'a matter of immediate urgency and permanent importance' and were supposed to 'shoot as well as possible and ride decently'. Acting as scouts and as rapid response forces they were to be one of the more successful innovations of the war. At the end of February 1st Gordons was again in action at the Battle of Paardeberg, fighting in 19 Brigade with 2nd Duke of Cornwall's Light Infantry, 2nd King's Shropshire Light Infantry and the Royal Canadian Regiment under the command of Brigadier-General Horace Smith-Dorrien. (Having become detached, B Company served in the Highland Brigade, which made the initial assault under its new commander Hector Macdonald, fresh from his exploits in Sudan where he had played a leading role at the Battle of Omdurman in 1898.) During the battle the attacking British and Canadian battalions made a frontal attack on the Boer positions and once again they were pinned down by accurate rifle fire. This time they did not lose their heads and the victory at Paardeberg helped to break the back of Boer resistance.

The victory and the surrender of Boer leader Piet Cronje was the turn of the tide and the war entered a new phase with the invasion of the Orange Free State and the Transvaal. During this phase 1st Gordons continued in Smith-Dorrien's 19 Brigade and with it took part in the advance across the Vaal towards Bloemfontein, which fell on 15 March. Then it was on to Pretoria, this time in a new force of 15,000 dubbed the Winburg Column and commanded by Hamilton, who had been given the temporary local rank of lieutenant-general. In a short but sharp action at the end of April at Houtnek on the road to Winburg Captain Ernest Towse led his men in a gallant charge on the slopes of Mount Thaba even though he had been shot in the face and blinded. He was awarded the Victoria Cross for this action and for an earlier act of bravery during the fighting at Magersfontein (see Appendix). By then Hamilton had crossed the River Vaal, the Boer's Rubicon, and the way to Johannesburg and Pretoria was open.

One obstacle remained in the way and its name is synonymous with the story of the Gordons in the Boer War – Doornkop, an entrenched Boer position on the Rand close to Johannesburg, where Jameson had been forced to surrender five years earlier. For Hamilton this was almost as important as Majuba and he was determined to take it even though it meant mounting a frontal attack which could be costly in casualties. It was the last set-piece battle of the war and a watching British officer serving with Rimington's Tigers, an irregular mounted infantry force, described the Gordons' charge on 29 May as the 'finest performance' he had seen throughout the campaign. In a sense it was, but it came at a heavy price. The Gordons swept up the hillside under murderous fire and lost over 100 men in the first ten minutes but the weight of their charge and the arrival of artillery support saw them reach the skyline where they charged into the position with the bayonet. As dusk fell Hamilton rode up the hill and thanked the 1st battalion: 'Men of the Gordons, officers of the Gordons, I want to tell you how proud I am of you, of my father's old regiment, and of the regiment I was born in. You have done splendidly.' What added lustre to the moment was that many of the men serving in the battalion were 128 Volunteers of M (1st Volunteer) Company, part-time soldiers who had answered the regiment's call for reinforcements. Two other Volunteer companies served in 2nd Gordons and a 4th Volunteer Company arrived in April 1902.

To all intents and purposes the war was now almost over. The main Boer strongholds were in British possession, the lines of communication had been secured and the Boer leadership was fractured but the fighting was destined to last another 18 months in its third and final phase, which involved both the Gordons battalions in the long and arduous mopping-up operations. At the end of the year, 1900, Roberts handed over command to General (later Field Marshal Lord) Kitchener, who had made his name commanding the forces in the Sudan campaign, but instead of tying up the loose ends the new commander-in-chief found himself engaged in a lengthy and bitter guerrilla war with an enemy who refused to give up the fight: most of the veldt was still free and the guerrillas made it their home, using deception, speed and marksmanship in place of fortification and artillery. With his army stretched out along the main lines of communication Kitchener decided to turn the position to his own advantage. He began by ordering a series of drives across the country to sweep the Boers out of their hiding places. It was a time-consuming exercise which tried the patience and the endurance of the British Army; the terrain militated against the methods and huge effort might only be rewarded by a handful of prisoners plus greater numbers of cattle and oxen.

The war was brought to a conclusion in May 1902 by the Treaty of Vereeniging and 1st Gordons began demobilising its reservists in preparation for returning home to be based at Glasgow's Maryhill Barracks, a part of Glasgow which the regimental historian described as being 'surrounded by mean streets'. Two years later the battalion moved to Cork which was described as a 'pleasant station' and this was 1st Gordons' home until September 1907 when it returned to Britain, this time to Maida Barracks at Aldershot, the so-called 'Home of the British Army'. October 1910 saw the battalion at Goojerat Barracks in Colchester where the soldiers found that dining halls had been introduced to end the practice of eating in barrack rooms. At the time the battalion was only 16 under its full complement of 783 and the records show that 207 were natives of the regiment's recruiting area while the majority, 234, came from the main cities, with only 80 being English. Three years later 1st Gordons made its final pre-war move when the battalion joined 8th Infantry Brigade at Plymouth where the soldiers found that the barracks waiting for them were only 'tolerably clean'.

2ND BATTALION

During the long period of home service which followed amalgamation the 2nd battalion was stationed in Edinburgh (1882–84), Devonport (1884–85), Guernsey (1885–87), Ireland (1887–94). In 1894 2nd Gordons moved to Maryhill Barracks in Glasgow where the 100th anniversary of the Gordons' formation was celebrated and new colours were presented by the Duke of Richmond and Gordon, great-grandson of the founder. Three years later the battalion took part in the celebrations for the sixtieth year of Queen Victoria's reign, which was marked by a huge parade in London featuring regiments from all over the British Empire. During this period of relative inactivity several officers took the opportunity of serving elsewhere, amongst them Ian Hamilton, at that time a captain, who joined the staff of the army in Egypt, and Hector Macdonald who commanded a Sudanese battalion. It was not until 1898 that 2nd Gordons was ordered to leave for India to replace 1st Gordons and as we have seen, the two battalions met at

Deolali as the former was arriving and the latter was in the process of leaving. Within a year the deteriorating situation in South Africa took the 2nd battalion to Natal and on arrival during the first week of October the men found that they were amongst friends. In command of the forces at Ladysmith was George White, now knighted and a lieutenant-general, and their brigade commander was Ian Hamilton.

The first battle of the war was fought at Talana on 19 October and although it was a narrow victory for the British it left Ladysmith exposed and led to a fresh pitched battle two days later at Elandslaagte, which involved 1st Manchesters, 1st Devonshires and 2nd Gordons. It was also a cavalry battle with 5th Dragoon Guards, 5th Lancers and squadrons of the Imperial Light Horse under the command of Major-General (later Field Marshal Lord) John French. For Hamilton this was a key moment: not only did he have his old regiment under his command but it was an opportunity to avenge Majuba Hill and he lost no time in reminding his men that the time had arrived to gain revenge. 'We'll do it, sir, we'll do it!' was the ready response. It was not an easy location – the actual battlefield consisted of a plain surrounded by a horseshoe of low hills – and the Boers were well dug in. At first the attack went well but 2nd Gordons soon found that their men made conspicuous targets. Although the Gordons had taken care to camouflage themselves with khaki kilt covers and by covering their brasses with dung, the green of their kilts was still visible and casualties began mounting, including the commanding officer, Lieutenant-Colonel W.H. Dick-Cunyngham, who had been awarded the Victoria Cross in Afghanistan. At this point Hamilton arrived on the scene on horseback and gave the order to fix bayonets and charge. Drum-Major Lawrence struck up 'The Haughs of Cromdale', the Devonshire's buglers responded and with shouts of 'Remember Majuba!' the British infantrymen went into the attack. Soon a white flag was seen over the Boer laager and although this suddenly vanished and the fighting resumed it did not take long to subdue the enemy's resistance. Elandslaagte was a notable victory, but it did not ease White's position in Ladysmith. Surrounded by Boer commandos the 13,000-strong garrison, including 2nd Gordons, was now under siege and despite reckless efforts to break out it lasted until February the following year.

In the next phase of the war 2nd Gordons formed 7th Brigade in the 4th Division, which was part of the Natal Field Force. With them they were involved in the operations to secure Natal between March and August and took part in actions at Witkoppies and Rooi Koppies before the fighting at Belfast, Lydenburg and Paardeplatts, which more or less brought the fighting to an end. Much of the effort involved lengthy marches and due to the fluctuations in temperatures – hot days and cold nights – the men carried the following kit: waterproof sheet, cardigan and warm cap while two blankets, serge trews, one spare shirt, one spare pair of socks, towel and washing materials were carried for each man on the battalion transport wagons. While on the march there was a unusual occurrence in September when the two battalions met. The incident was recorded by Major (later General Sir) C.E. Calwell in the November 1900 issue of *Blackwood's Magazine*:

> Out of the darkness strode a long column of kilted men and the Gordons all round us were hastening towards it in a great humming eager swarm, officers and men jostling one another, discipline and ceremony cast aside, for a great moment had come in the history of a renowned regiment. The old 75th, with its Dargai laurels scarcely faded, who had fought at Magersfontein and Paardeberg, were meeting the 92nd who had come from Ladysmith, on a scene of victory amid mountains such as rear their heads in distant

> Aberdeenshire. For a few minutes the upland buzzed with eager conversation, anxious questions, cheery greetings, uproarious laughter.

At the end of the war 2nd Gordons returned to India and between 1902 and 1909 the battalion was stationed variously at Sialkot, Peshawar, Calcutta and Cawnpore. A highlight was the battalion's participation in the famous Delhi Durbar of 1911 when it supplied the guard of honour to King George V, its colonel-in-chief. The posting lasted until the end of 1912, when the battalion received orders to move to Cairo, where it moved into the Kasr-el-Nil barracks. This was to be home for the next year and a half, a period of calm when as the regimental historian wryly noted 'life was quiet until the crisis burst'.

Of the Gordons who fought in the Boer War and rose to prominence during it, White was invalided home after Ladysmith and was later promoted field marshal. He died in 1912, having served as Governor of the Royal Hospital in Chelsea. Hamilton's star continued to shine – he became Inspector-General of the Overseas Forces – but his career virtually ended in 1915, when he was made the scapegoat for the failure of the Gallipoli operations during the First World War. Macdonald, too, should have gone on to greater things. He was knighted, promoted major-general and given command of the garrison in Ceylon but in March 1903 he took his life in a hotel room in Paris rather than face a court martial on charges which have never been substantiated but may have involved sexual relations with young boys.

SIX

The First World War: The Western Front 1914–16

In the early summer of 1914 Europe was rocked by a succession of events which would plunge the world into its first global conflict and the first major European war since 1815. It all began innocuously in June, when the Archduke Franz Ferdinand, heir to the throne of Austria-Hungary, was killed together with his wife during a state visit to Sarajevo, the capital of Bosnia-Herzegovina. At first the news made little impact in Britain and initial reports suggested that the perpetrators would be apprehended and punished – the general opinion was that even if war did break out it would only be a local affair – but when it became clear that neighbouring Serbia might have been implicated in the attack the crisis deepened. On 23 July, weeks after the assassination, Austria-Hungary issued an ultimatum to Serbia making ten demands for the suppression of Serb nationalist groups, the punishment of the assassins and participation in the judicial process. Serbia was given 48 hours to comply and although the response was placatory its government stopped short of allowing Austria-Hungary to take part in the trial of the assassins, arguing that the matter should be referred to the International Court at The Hague. That readiness to cooperate seemed to settle the matter, but already diplomacy was proving powerless to stop Europe's drift towards war. Both countries mobilised their armed forces when Germany, Austria-Hungary's main ally, encouraged Vienna to take decisive action against the Serbs before any other country intervened in the crisis. Confident of German support Austria-Hungary declared war on Serbia five days after issuing its first demands, thus paving the way for a wider conflict. The following day, 29 July, Russia, Serbia's traditional friend and protector, began to deploy its forces along the border with Austria and within 24 hours this was followed by the order for full mobilisation.

Although the move was made to discourage Austria-Hungary it threatened Germany, which immediately demanded that Russia 'cease every war measure against us and Austria-Hungary'. On 1 August Germany declared war on Russia, followed two days later by a further declaration of war against France, Russia's ally. That same day German forces began crossing into Belgium as part of a pre-arranged strategy called the Schlieffen Plan, to bypass the heavily fortified French frontier and encircle Paris from the north through Belgium. Britain, which had wanted to remain aloof from the crisis and was not formally in alliance with any of the main participants, was now about to be pressed into the conflict through a treaty of 1839 which guaranteed Belgium's neutrality. On 4 August, no answer having been received to a demand that Belgium should remain unmolested, Britain declared war on Germany. As part of the 'Precautionary Period' of the Defence Plan Prior to Mobilisation, formations of the Regular Army based in Britain were told to return to their depots on 29 July. Most were on their annual summer camps or undergoing live firing exercises. At the outbreak of war 1st Gordon Highlanders was based at Plymouth where it formed part of 8 Brigade in the 3rd Division, while the 2nd battalion was based in Cairo. Later, on its deployment to France, the latter battalion would serve with 20 Brigade in the 7th Division. The British-based battalions crossed over to France with the first elements of the British Expeditionary Force (BEF) in the third week of August, while the overseas-based battalions arrived in France from September onwards.

At the outbreak of war Field Marshal Lord Kitchener was appointed Secretary for War and at his first Cabinet meeting he astonished his colleagues by claiming that the war would last for a minimum of three years and would require over one million men to win it. On 8 August the call went out for the first 100,000 volunteers who would form the first of the New Armies. Kitchener's methods were as controversial as his prognosis was pessimistic. Instead of making immediate use of the part-time soldiers of the Territorial Force which had been raised for home defence in 1908 he decided to build on the existing regimental structure of the British Regular Army. No new formations would be raised but the existing infantry regiments would increase the numbers of their battalions to meet the demand for men. These would be known as 'special service battalions' and the men who joined them would volunteer for the duration of the war. In that way, argued Kitchener, the volunteers could be assimilated quickly into the 'New' or 'Kitchener' armies and no new machinery would have to be assembled to deal with them. Although Kitchener placed little faith in the soldiers of the Territorial Force, dismissing them as a 'town clerk's army' full of sky-larkers, the existing battalions were allowed to volunteer for service overseas. Once introduced on 13 August the idea caught on and group pressure made it difficult for serving Territorials to refuse to serve overseas if the majority of the battalion volunteered. All the first-line Territorial battalions of The Gordon Highlanders served abroad, in France and on the Western Front. Unusually, the

Gordons did not serve on the other main battlefronts – Gallipoli, Palestine, Mesopotamia and Salonika – although, as we shall see, 2nd Gordon Highlanders had the distinction of being part of the British and French forces sent to assist the Italians in the autumn of 1917 following their heavy defeat by Austro-German forces at Caporetto and the subsequent collapse of the home government.

During the period 1914–19 the Gordons expanded considerably to produce the following Regular, Territorial and Special Service battalions:

1st Battalion, 8th Brigade, 3rd Division, Plymouth
2nd Battalion, Cairo
3rd (Reserve) Battalion, Aberdeen
1/4th (City of Aberdeen) Battalion (Territorial Force), Aberdeen
2/4th (City of Aberdeen) Battalion (Territorial Force), Aberdeen
3/4th (City of Aberdeen) Battalion (Territorial Force), Aberdeen
1/5th (Buchan and Formartine) Battalion (Territorial Force), Peterhead
2/5th (Buchan and Formartine) Battalion (Territorial Force), Peterhead
3/5th (Buchan and Formartine) Battalion (Territorial Force), Peterhead
1/6th (Banffshire and Donside) Battalion (Territorial Force), Keith
2/6th (Banffshire and Donside) Battalion (Territorial Force), Keith
3/6th (Banffshire and Donside) Battalion (Territorial Force), Keith
1/7th (Deeside) Battalion, (Territorial Force), Banchory

The Duchess of Gordon raising The Gordon Highlanders, 1794.
(Watercolour by W.S. Cumming.)

Major-General Robert Abercromby of Tullibody, who raised the 75th Highlanders in 1787.
(Reproduced in oil from a painting by Henry Raeburn.)

The 75th Highlanders take part in the successful storming of Seringapatam on 22 February 1792.
(Lithograph published by Robert Ker Porter and John P. Thompson, 1802.)

The death of Colonel John Cameron of Fassiefern at Quatre Bras, 1815.
(Watercolour by R. Simkin.)

Gordons and Greys to the front.
(Reproduction lithograph by S. Berkeley.)

The storming of the Asmai Heights by the 92nd Highlanders in 1879.
(Oil painting by W.S. Cumming.)

The 1st battalion in action in the Malakand Pass during the Chitral campaign of 1895.
(Oil painting by S.W. Lincoln.)

Piper George Findlater wins the Victoria Cross during the storming of the Heights of Dargai on the North-West Frontier in 1897.
(Oil painting by V.M. Hamilton.)

Men of the 1st battalion in action during the Battle of Magersfontein in December 1899, one of the early battles of the Boer War. (Watercolour by F. Feller.)

Three officers of the 1st battalion photographed in France during the early months of the First World War. Note that they are carrying their broadswords without the basket.

Men of the Gordon Highlanders on the march in France in 1914.
As was the custom, the commanding officer is mounted.

Colonel Alistair Gordon, 2nd Gordons, wounded and awaiting evacuation during the Battle of Festubert in 1915.

Territorial soldiers of 5/7th Gordons practise shooting at an 'enemy' aircraft at Dreghorn during the annual summer camp, around 1937.

Drums and pipes of the Gordons march through Chipping Campden in 1944.

During the Burma campaign, 8th Gordons served in the anti-aircraft and anti-tank role with the Royal Artillery. Officers photographed at a planning meeting.

Officer of 1st Gordons with local villagers during the 'emergency' in Malaya in the early 1950s.

In the mid-1960s, 1st Gordons served on the eastern seaboard of Sabah during the confrontation in Borneo. A goat joins the proceedings.

In his role as colonel-in-chief of The Gordon Highlanders, H.R.H. Prince Charles, Prince of Wales and Duke of Rothesay, attends the final Trooping of the Colour at Seaton Park in Aberdeen on 25 June 1994.

2/7th (Deeside) Battalion (Territorial Force), Banchory

3/7th (Deeside) Battalion (Territorial Force), Banchory

8th (Service) Battalion (New Army), Aberdeen

9th (Service) Battalion (New Army), Aberdeen

10th (Service) Battalion (New Army), Aberdeen

11th (Reserve) Battalion (New Army), Aberdeen

1st Garrison Battalion (New Army), India (1916)

Mention must also be made of the regiment's association with The London Scottish, which served in the Territorial Force as 14th (County of London) Battalion, The London Regiment (London Scottish). Consisting mainly of Scots living in the London area, it was raised originally in 1859 and before the 1908 Haldane reforms was allotted to The Rifle Brigade as one of its Volunteer battalions. As 1/14th London Regiment it was the first Territorial Force battalion to cross over to France in 1914 and saw action during the First Battle of Ypres, where it lost 750 casualties (killed, wounded or missing). Amongst the survivors was the future Hollywood film star Ronald Colman. In 1916 The London Scottish became part of the Gordons and its 2/14th battalion served later in Salonika and Palestine.

As was the case in every part of Britain, the north-east was not slow to volunteer for the duration of the war, and by the autumn the Gordons had raised four special service battalions: 8th, 9th, 10th and 11th. At the same time the regiment's four Territorial battalions – 1/4th, 1/5th, 1/6th and 1/7th – all volunteered for service overseas and were soon serving in France. In July all were engaged on their annual summer camps and for all the men the transition from weekend soldiering to serving in an operational division was to be a bewildering experience. It is impossible to think of a better example of the outpouring of patriotism that helped to create the volunteer army than to recount the experience of the men of U company which formed part of the $1/4^{th}$ Battalion (City of Aberdeen) The Gordon Highlanders (Territorial Force). At the time that Europe was slowly descending into war it was finishing its annual two-week camp at Tain on the shores of the Dornoch Firth with 'a huge bonfire around which the volunteer soldiers held a sing-song fuelled by some bottles of beer'. The following day, 30 July, came news of the general mobilisation and the 132 soldiers of U Company, all students or graduates of Aberdeen University, found themselves on the verge of going off to war. To make matters worse, it began raining and the special train taking them home had to be cancelled.

The men of U Company were part-time soldiers in the Territorial Force which had been formed in 1908 as a second line for home defence and provided one of the eight (later four) rifle companies of the local Territorial battalion, $1/4^{th}$ Gordon Highlanders. As its historian has recorded, its association with Aberdeen University meant that the men were very much the Scottish nation in uniform: 'Although the majority of its members were from Aberdeen and the North-East, students from Caithness and the Lothians served in the ranks with Gaelic speakers from the Hebrides and the Western Isles.' One of their number, Alexander Rule, remembered that they were happy enough to embrace mobilisation provided that they could retain 'the original title of a University Unit which, even after months of heavy trench warfare in the Ypres salient, sang *Gaudeamus* to the end'. Before it left for France, U Company was designated D Company, $1/4^{th}$ Gordon Highlanders, when the battalion's original eight companies were regrouped as double companies to meet army requirements but within the battalion and amongst its own members it kept its old title and took great pride in the fact that it consisted of 'student soldiers'.

1914

The Western Front: 1st, 2nd, 1/6th battalions

The first Gordons to see action were the regulars of the 1st and 2nd battalions. As soon as war had been declared 532 reservists had left Aberdeen to join 1st Gordons in Plymouth, where they came under the command of Lieutenant-Colonel F.H. Neish. On 13 August the battalion crossed over to France and joined the British Expeditionary Force (BEF) at Hyon near Mons. The role of the BEF had been agreed before the war but by the time it deployed in support of the French Fifth Army on the northern end of the French line the situation was changing day by day. The German attack into France and Belgium was based on the pre-war Schlieffen Plan, the Germans' operational plan to knock out France quickly and decisively, which had been drawn up in 1905 by the Chief of the General Staff Field Marshal Alfred von Schlieffen and then much modified by his successor, Helmuth von Moltke. When the attack began the French underestimated its strength and a counter-attack into the Ardennes was quickly repulsed. To make matters worse, on 22 August General Lanzerac's Fifth Army was defeated on the Sambre, with the loss of over 4,000 casualties. The setback forced him to withdraw, leaving the BEF isolated in its defensive positions on the Mons–Conde canal with I Corps deployed to the east and II Corps stretched out along a 20-mile front to the west. Bearing down on them from the north were six divisions of General Alexander von Kluck's First Army. Field Marshal Sir John French, the British commander-in-chief, agreed to hold the position for 24 hours and his men began digging in for the expected onslaught, using the features of the mining area with its spoil heaps and buildings to enhance their defences.

The expected German assault began on the morning of 23 August and for the attacking enemy infantrymen it was a sobering experience. Trained to fire 15 rifle rounds a minute, the British regiments poured their fire into the advancing German lines with predictable results – the rate was so rapid and concentrated that the Germans believed they were facing machine-gun fire. By the end of the day the attack had faltered as exhausted and frightened Germans attempted to regroup, but despite halting the assault the BEF was obliged to retire and in the coming days its regiments were to receive increasingly high casualties. (The exact numbers are impossible to compute as War Diaries were written up later and information about casualties was of necessity incomplete.) The Great Retreat towards the River Marne, as it was known, would take the German Army to the outskirts of Paris and the BEF suffered further casualties on 26 August when II Corps turned to face the advancing Germans at Le Cateau, some 30 miles from Mons. It was the British Army's biggest set-piece battle since Waterloo and its 55,000 soldiers faced a German opposition which numbered 140,000. Lieutenant-General Sir Horace Smith-Dorrien's II Corps was able to hold the line by dint of superior firepower, but by evening the British were outnumbered and only a German failure to press home their advantage allowed the British to resume their retreat. Even so, the casualties were heavy – 7,812 killed – and gave a stark indication of worse things to come. Exhausted by the battle and the summer heat the BEF continued to pull back amid rumours that the war was lost and that the French government had evacuated Paris for Bordeaux. It was a time of confusion, when the fog of war seemed very real indeed as the battle-weary infantrymen continued to sleepwalk – as it seemed – through the French countryside.

It was during this mobile and disorienting stage of the battle that disaster hit 1st Gordons. In the confusion of the retreat some battalions became isolated and were unaware of the orders coming down from brigade or divisional headquarters. That was the predicament facing 1st Gordon Highlanders on the night of

25 August as 8 Brigade covered the 3rd Division's retreat from Le Cateau. With the exception of A Company the battalion found itself isolated at Caudry, together with elements of 2nd Royal Scots and 1st Royal Irish as the rest of the brigade, unknown to them, withdrew. Colonel Neish was disinclined to retreat without receiving orders but his second-in-command urged him to see sense and order a withdrawal. The subordinate's warning carried weight: Major & Brevet Colonel William Eagleson Gordon was not only superior in army rank but had been awarded the Victoria Cross during the Boer War at Krugersdorp, where his gallantry under fire saved the British guns. A furious row broke out between the two men and Gordon exercised his right to take over command as the senior officer in charge of a mixed force of Gordons, Royal Scots and Royal Irish. The force started pulling out in the early hours of the morning but it was too late. On the outskirts of the village of Bertry the Germans were waiting, the Gordons were surrounded and in the confusion of night most of the men were either killed or taken prisoner and 500 survivors were forced to surrender. As a result, the battalion almost ceased to exist and had to be rebuilt with fresh recruits: all that was left of it was one rifle company of three platoons which had managed to withdraw from Le Cateau. The men involved in the incident were in an impossible position and the most reasonable comment was left to the *Official History* which drily remarked that 'the fortune of war was hard upon the 1/Gordons', adding the solace that their 'gallant resistance' had saved others during the retreat. Unfortunately, because there was confusion over the actual surrender, it was not the end of the matter. Gordon wanted to continue fighting, as did other officers, but Neish gave the order to surrender to avoid unnecessary casualties and the battle was refought after the war in an army board of investigation and a libel case instigated by Colonel Gordon.

At the end of September, 1st Gordons returned to 8 Brigade

and within the next fortnight it was joined in France by the arrival of 2nd Gordons which, together with 1st Grenadier Guards, 2nd Scots Guards and 2nd Border Regiment, formed 20 Brigade in 7th Division. (In December the 2nd battalion's brigade was reinforced by the arrival of 1/6th Gordons.) Both were in action during the First Battle of Ypres, which opened on 18 October with an advance towards the German lines at Menin. The fighting continued until 22 November and the actual battle consisted of various actions at Langemarck, Gheluvelt, La Bassée and Nonne Boschen, all of which are recognised on the regiment's list of battle honours (see Appendix). Some of the fiercest fighting on the Ypres salient took place at Gheluvelt and it was there that Captain Ortho Brooke won a posthumous Victoria Cross. (He was the son of Sir Harry Brooke of Colebrooke in Ulster, a well-known Gordon Highlander.) It was not the first VC awarded to the regiment – a few days earlier Drummer William Kenny had distinguished himself by rescuing wounded men under fire – but it came at a high cost to the regiment. During the action at Gheluvelt 2nd Gordons lost over 100 casualties killed but had the satisfaction of counting 240 dead Germans in front of one of their platoon's trenches. Some idea of the conditions facing the 7th Division at Ypres can be found in the diary of the 2nd Gordons' brigade commander Brigadier-General Reginald Heyworth, which is held by the Imperial War Museum:

> 14 December: A lot of rain in the night again. Went into the trenches at 8.30 a.m. and found them in an awful mess. There were 2 men killed when I was in the trenches. 1 Gordon and 1 Border, both shot through the head. I rode this afternoon with Palmer and we visited the headquarters of the Scots Guards, Border and 6 Gordons. We met the two companies of the 6 Gordons coming out of the

> trenches and I have never seen men in such a state of mud and so tired. I am afraid they will not be very good anyway at present. They are very young and this trench work completely beats them.

For the British it was the first great killing battle of the war. Although the BEF stemmed the German attack it paid a heavy price: 8,631 officers and men had been killed, 37,264 were wounded and 40,342 were missing. By then the Regular Army battalions were being joined by the soldiers of the Territorial Force and the New Armies. In the first week of December, in response to the need for massive reinforcement, Kitchener had sanctioned the deployment of the first 23 battalions from the Territorial Force. Amongst them was 1/6th Gordons and it was followed by 1/4th Gordons in February the following year. Both joined a front which had not been foreseen by the pre-war planners: a pattern of trenches which ran from the Channel coast to the frontier with Switzerland as all hope of attacking vulnerable flanks disappeared. When 1914 drew to an end the Western Front, as it would be known, was quiet as the three armies took stock of the situation, regrouped and restocked their depleted supplies of men, stores and ammunition.

1915
The Western Front: 1st, 2nd, 1/4th, 1/5th, 1/6th, 1/7th, 8th, 9th, 10th battalions

The strategic situation at the start of the second year of the war was dominated by the stalemate on the Western Front, where the soldiers were having to come to terms with the reality of warfare in the trenches. The conditions might have been basic, occasionally unsanitary and frequently verminous, but the trench system offered safety to its inhabitants, with a complicated system of underground shelters, support and communication trenches protected by breastworks and barbed wire. Between them and the German line lay no-man's-land, a space of open ground which could be as wide as 300 yards or as narrow as 25 yards. From the air it looked orderly and secure, but the creation of the trench system also dominated the tactics used by both sides and would scarcely change until the return to more open warfare in the last months of the war. In 1915 the dilemma facing British and French planners was how to break the German trench line by attacking key points which would force the enemy to fall back on its lines of communication and in so doing return some fluidity to the fighting. Lines of advance had to be chosen and in January the Allies agreed to mount offensives against both sides of the German salient, which ran from Flanders to Verdun. These would be made at Aubers Ridge and Vimy Ridge to the north and in Champagne to the south, the intention being to squeeze the Germans and perhaps even converge to complete the encirclement of the salient. In this Spring Offensive the British and the French would attack in Flanders and Artois, the French alone in the Champagne. For the British this would involve them in battles at Neuve Chapelle, Aubers Ridge and Festubert, and later in the year at Loos. All failed to achieve the Allies' objectives and all produced large numbers of casualties.

The first battle, Neuve Chapelle, was initiated by Field Marshal French to win back a German salient captured in October 1914. This position gave the Germans the freedom to fire on British positions from both flanks and the danger had to be eliminated, but French also hoped to exploit any success by threatening the German lines of communication between La Bassée and Lille. The plan was to attack on a narrow front of only 2,000 yards using four infantry brigades in the initial assault phase. When the attack began at 7.30 a.m. on 10 March it achieved complete surprise. The huge British bombardment also encouraged the waiting infantrymen to believe that no one could have survived the shelling and when they began their attack half an hour later hopes were high that an early breakthrough could be achieved. In the 20 Brigade attack 2nd Gordons were on the left flank with 1st Grenadier Guards on the right.

There was further fighting the following day and on 12 March there was a renewed attack to try to break out of Neuve Chapelle but by then the battle was already slipping out of the hands of the British commanders. Communications between the front lines and rear areas broke down quickly and decisively. There was no radio or telephone link and messages had to be sent by runners, with the result that the assault formations were unable to make contact with headquarters. For the battalion commanders this proved to be fatal, as orders were painfully slow to get to the front lines or did not arrive at all, with the result that there was a complete collapse in command and control. Initially taken by surprise, the Germans responded with a will, and rushed reinforcements into the line and were soon in a position to counter-attack. However, these assaults failed to make any headway, due to the fact that the British forces had also been able to regroup their defensive lines and when the battle was finally called off that evening the losses on both sides were high – the British lost 11,652 casualties killed, wounded or taken prisoner and the Germans an estimated 8,500. Amongst the British casualties 2nd and 1/6th Gordons lost 525 casualties, killed, wounded or missing. In addition, the two Gordons battalions lost their commanding officers, both killed on the same day, 13 March: Lieutenant-Colonel Henry Uniacke, 2nd Gordons who had been wounded at Ypres and Lieutenant-Colonel Colin McLean, 1/6th Gordons, a veteran who had been with the battalion since it was first embodied for war service.

Two months later both battalions were involved in a more ambitious assault against the German lines at Aubers Ridge. Once more the failure to cut the wire caused high British casualties as the infantry made their way over the unpromising terrain towards the

German positions and 458 officers and 11,161 other ranks were lost during three days of fighting. Of these, 280 were officers and men of the Gordons, killed, wounded or missing. During the battle 2nd Gordons witnessed a curious incident when German artillery opened fire on its own infantry during the 20 Brigade attack on 17 May. Only later did it become clear that the German gunners were doing this deliberately, to prevent their own men surrendering. A substantial number of them were taken prisoner by 1/6th Gordons. By then the three Gordons battalions on the Western Front had been joined by 8th Gordons serving in the 9th (Scottish) Division, 9th and 10th Gordons serving in the 15th (Scottish) Division, the former in the pioneer role, and 1/5th and 1/7th Gordons in the 51st (Highland) Division. (Later in the war 1/6th Gordons would transfer to the Highland Division, serving in 152 Brigade.)

With the exception of the two Territorial battalions in the Highland Division, all the Gordons battalions took part in the Battle of Loos, which opened on 25 September before it petered out early in the following month. In strategic terms it was a meaningless battle. The attacking divisions gained a salient two miles deep and in the early stages of the battle some Scottish battalions had the heady sensation of advancing steadily across no-man's-land, but the end result did little to help the French offensive in Artois and Champagne, the main reason why the battle took place. From the outset, the planning for the battle was a story of improvisation and optimism that the weight of the French attack would lead to an early breakthrough, thereby taking some of the strain off the attacking divisions. The plan was for the British First Army to attack from its lines in the north along a wide front that stretched from a position known as the Hohenzollern Redoubt to the town of Loos, while the French would strike at the German defensive positions on the Vimy Ridge and further south, in Champagne.

General Sir Douglas Haig, who had succeeded Field Marshal French as commander-in-chief, counted on surprise and placed great hope on the use of chlorine gas, which would be released from cylinders but depended on a favourable wind blowing it towards the German lines. The plan was to unleash the gas at first light, following an artillery bombardment which would increase in intensity, and then to attack with six divisions in line along a broad front. In view of what happened – Loos was not a success – it is tempting to write off the battle as a futile waste of the lives of men who were ill-prepared to face the shock of modern warfare. Certainly, in the aftermath of the war that was how Loos came to be viewed, but at the time the soldiers had a good conceit of themselves and their ability to take on the enemy. As 1/6th Gordons waited in the front-line trenches on the eve of battle one of their officers, Alick Buchanan-Smith, noted the stoicism of his men as they waited for the battle to begin:

> Quite clearly they were a happy lot and very confident that the battle which lay ahead would see the rout of the Kaiser and his troops. Impatient for the battle to start but with little apprehension or anxiety for themselves, however much each one may have felt it in his bones. Most of them had made their wills in one form or another.

Also taking part in another subsidiary brigade attack to the north, at Hooge, undertaken by 3rd Division, were the student soldiers of 1/4th Gordons who had provided an intellectual diversion by starting an informal debating club known as 'The Jocks' Society'. As one of its members, Robert Stewart, wrote later in the university magazine *Alma Mater*, it held its final meeting on the evening of 22 September over a simple meal of potatoes and meat sauce:

> Those of us who were privileged to attend will recall the scene – Sergeant Crichton in the presidential chair maintained order with zest in debates. The speeches of such as Privates Mason and Surtees were received with keen relish, and appreciated as literary delicacies by their hearers, while Peterkin's caustic humour, usually directed against some members of the Society, and Sunny's [McLellan] subtlety added greatly to the enjoyment of the evening.
>
> Supper over, we gathered round the hearth of the open fireplace and the past occupied our thoughts. Marischal College, with all its joys and associations, was discussed, and many a wish expressed that soon, notebook in hand, we would again cross the quadrangle. No mention of the morrow was made.

Their fate, and the fate of all the Gordons soldiers at Loos, would soon be known. In the early hours of the morning on 25 September as the roar of the artillery grew to a crescendo the first gas was discharged in advance of the first attacks. In some sectors it drifted listlessly towards the German lines on the soft south-westerly wind but to the north it blew back on the lines of the 2nd Division causing it to halt its attack along both banks of the La Bassée Canal. Its role was to provide flanking cover for the 9th (Scottish) Division's attack on the formidable obstacle of the Hohenzollern Redoubt and Fosse 8 where the German observation posts were sited. Further to the south the attack of the 15th (Scottish) Division was more successful and by 8.00 a.m. Loos was in British hands although the next objective, Hill 70, was fiercely contested by the German defenders.

By midday there was optimism in the British ranks. The German line had been broken and there were reports of panic in Lens where the headquarters of the German Sixth Army was making preparations to pull out. In some places there had been little opposition, a result of the gas and sustained bombardment, but already the Germans were rushing their reserves into the line and fighting hard to protect key points such as Hill 70 and the Hohenzollern Redoubt. Everything now depended on the deployment of the reserve divisions and the renewal of accurate artillery fire to support the units which were still engaged with the Germans. At Hill 70 the Scottish battalions were pinned down on the forward slopes by German machine-gun fire and were forced to dig in. The gains made on the first day of the battle were the high-water mark for the British divisions at Loos. Now was the time to deploy the reserves but it was at this point that Haig's plan began to unravel. Before midday the three reserve divisions – Guards, 21st and 24th (the latter two both inexperienced New Army divisions) – were ordered to deploy, but it took time for them to make their way to the front and by the time they assembled between Loos and the Hulluch–Vermelles road on the morning of 26 September they were tired and hungry. Overcrowding in the rear of the British line had added to their difficulties, the roads were heavily congested and in some sectors units were forced to bypass British obstacles, compounding the confusion. At the same time the Germans had been busy reinforcing their own positions and by the time the two reserve New Army divisions began their attack they were met with sustained machine-gun and artillery fire and by nightfall on 27 September any hope of a successful 'Big Push' had evaporated.

Bowing to the demands of the French Haig kept the battle going in the British sector until October 16, by which time the British casualties at Loos and the subsidiary attacks amounted to 2,466 officers and 59,247 other ranks. It has been estimated that of the 20,598 names on the memorial to the missing at Loos, one in three is Scots. The memorial surrounds the graves at Dud Corner on the Loos–Vermelles road, where the old British front line ran and from which the 15th Scottish Division attacked; it was unveiled on 4 August 1930, fittingly by a Gordon Highlander, General Sir Nevil Macready. Of those casualties, killed, wounded or missing, 2,066 were Gordon Highlanders. Amongst them were 104 men of D (or U) Company, 1/4th Gordons, who became casualties while attacking the German positions at Hooge on the Ypres Salient as part of a diversionary attack to the north of the Loos battlefield. As a result the company of student soldiers ceased to exist in its earlier form and was changed inexorably by the arrival of new drafts and the transfer of many of the survivors to serve in other battalions. The battalion suffered 334 casualties 'as far as is known', recorded the adjutant and he was right to be circumspect. After the battle a Gordons officer saw six men under the command of a junior NCO and asked why they were not marching as a platoon. 'Platoon?' came the reply. 'This is D Company.'

1916
The Western Front: 1st, 2nd, 1/4th, 1/5th, 1/6th, 1/7th, 8/10th, 9th battalions

The third year of the war was dominated by the Battle of the Somme, which began on the first day of July and eventually drew to a close in November, when fierce winter weather made further fighting impossible. For many people it is one of the defining actions of the war, remembered as much for the carnage it created as for its lack of tactical success. Instead of creating the great breakthrough, as the high command hoped, the Somme was to be remembered as the killing ground of the British Army – no other battlefield of the First World War created more casualties per square yard and the opening day of the battle, 1 July 1916, was to produce the bloodiest day for the infantry regiments which took part in the initial attack. From the eleven divisions which began the assault, 57,470 men became casualties – 21,392 killed or missing, 35,493 wounded and 585 taken prisoner. It would take another 140 days before the fighting in the sector finally came to an end.

Amongst the battalions in action in the first hours of the battle was 2nd Gordons, which had the melancholy distinction of taking part in 7th Division's assault against Mametz, described as 'a miniature fortress' on the right of the British line. In the first minutes as the battalion attacked towards Fricourt 9th Devonshires on the left ran into uncut wire and its men were mown down by German machine guns which had not been destroyed during the British artillery barrage. The Gordons' losses were high – 16 officers and 445 soldiers out of the 24 officers and 783 soldiers who had gone into the attack but as the battalion had achieved the objectives given it was considered a successful attack. A diary kept by one of the officers, Captain (later Lieutenant-Colonel) R.A. Wolfe Murray, gives a rather different picture. Having blown his whistle at zero hour Wolfe Murray took D Company into the attack, carrying his walking stick, his men with their rifles at the high port, just as Wellington's men had done 100 years ago:

> The folly of such tactics were [*sic*] soon to be ghastly apparent, we were shot down like balls at a fair before ever we could cover the 200 yds separating us from the enemy's front line. Let it here be explained that this method of advance was forced upon us by those who feared that if men doubled they would disappear for ever and so a repetition of the battle of Loos would be enacted where nobody really knew the position of the advanced troops throughout the day, owing to every man having more or less gone hell for leather, as hard as he could, straight to his own front.

By the middle of July early hopes of a breakthrough had evaporated but the attack continued. On 14 July 1st Gordons was involved in the assault on Longueval and Delville Wood, where there was a danger that the Germans might counter-attack in strength. As the regimental historian of the war starkly reminds his readers, the battalion's experience was reduced to 'mud, gas hanging in the trees, uncertainty about the situation and disorganisation'. By then the Territorial battalions of the 51st (Highland) Division had joined the battle and their first experience of combat was to be uncomfortable, to say the least. Tasked to take High Wood (the French name is Bois des Forceaux, Raven Wood) and its neighbouring defences, the raw division ran into concentrated German machine-gun fire and suffered accordingly. The Highland Territorial battalions suffered 3,500 casualties following two attacks on the heavily defended German position, a situation which the divisional historian recorded as being 'disappointing and dispiriting to all'. Later in the summer 1st Gordons was part of the 3rd Division's attack at Guillemont and Ginchy on 18 August, 1/4th Gordons attacked over much the same ground three weeks later and the amalgamated 8/10th Gordons was part of 15th (Scottish) Division's attack at Martinpuich in the middle of September. Winter was fast approaching and by then, according to an officer quoted in the history of the 51st (Highland) Division, 'The country had become waterlogged owing to excessive downpours of rain. Continual mists and the absence of wind prevented the rain from being absorbed in the atmosphere. The ground thus remained sodden, the roads were reduced to a pulp, and tracks and paths became lost in oozing mud of the consistency of porridge.'

During the last phase of the battle, which dragged on until the middle of November, five battalions (1st, 2nd, 1/4th, 1/5th and 1/7th) took part in the fighting on the River Ancre and the actions at

Beaucourt and Beaumont Hamel. The attack was due to begin on 24 October but after many postponements finally commenced on 13 November with the explosion of a mine in front of the German lines and the customary artillery barrage. Under the command of Major-General George 'Uncle' Harper the 51st Highland Division attacked with two brigades and one in reserve, using 'leap-frog' tactics as they advanced towards the German lines of defence. On the right 1/7th Gordons and 1/6th Black Watch quickly reached the German front line and took it without difficulty and although 1/8th Argylls and 1/5th Seaforths were checked on the left, they were able to fight their way through to the second line. Harper's tactics worked in that the division achieved its objectives with only 2,200 casualties killed, wounded or missing.

Although the operation took place in January 1917 mention must be made of an audacious assault made by 8/10th Gordons on a German position known as the Butte de Warlencourt. A prehistoric burial ground which dominated the surrounding countryside, its mass of tunnels and trench systems made it a formidable obstacle which the Germans used for artillery spotting. On 29 January the battalion mounted a determined attack on the position, the soldiers wearing white smocks and whitewashed helmets as camouflage in the wintry conditions. For modest losses 8/10th Gordons took around 60 prisoners and succeeded in blowing up the German ammunition dump, a satisfactory ending to a daring raid.

SEVEN

The First World War: The Western Front and Italy 1917–19

In the cold statistical analysis of modern warfare the Allies had done better than the Germans out of the fighting on the Somme and with the benefit of hindsight it can be claimed as 'a win on points'. While the expected breakthrough never occurred and the ground gained was a modest return for the expenditure of so many lives, pressure had been taken off the French in the southern sectors and valuable lessons had been learned. After the war senior German commanders admitted that the Somme was 'the muddy grave of the German field army' while their opposite numbers in the British Army argued that the inexperienced New Army divisions had come of age during the battle, even though most of the lessons were bloodily learned.

The battle had also forced the enemy to reappraise their options. Rightly fearing the renewal of a bigger Allied offensive in the same sector in the new year the German high command decided to shorten the line between Arras and the Aisne by constructing new and heavily fortified defences which would be their new 'final' position behind the Somme battlefield. Known to the Germans as the Siegfried Stellung and to the Allies as the Hindenburg Line, this formidable construction shortened the Front by some 30 miles and created an obstacle which would not be taken until the end of the war. The withdrawal began on 16 March, and as the Germans retired they laid waste to the countryside leaving a devastated landscape in which the cautiously pursuing Allies had to build new trench systems. To meet this new challenge the Allies planned a new spring assault on the shoulders of the Somme salient, with the French attacking in the south at Chemin des Dames while the British and Canadians would mount a supporting offensive at Arras and Vimy Ridge. Prior to the British attack, which began on 9 April, there would be a huge and violent bombardment with 2,879 guns firing 2,687,000 shells over a five-day period.

1917

The Western Front: 1st, 2nd, 1/4th, 1/5th, 1/6th, 1/7th, 8/10th, 9th battalions

The Battle of Arras opened in atrocious weather conditions with a biting wind which sent snow flurries scudding across the countryside, but despite the wintry weather the portents were good. For the first time, the assault battalions found that the artillery had done its job by destroying the wire, and new types of gas shells had fallen in the rear areas, killing German transport horses and making the movement of guns impossible. Within a few hours the German line had been penetrated to a depth of two miles and in one of the most astonishing feats of the war the Canadian divisions captured the previously impregnable German positions on the gaunt features of Vimy Ridge. The first day of the assault was a triumph for the British and the Canadians, who suffered reasonably small casualties and succeeded in taking their first objectives and then regrouping to attack the second and third lines of defence. The successful first phase encouraged hopes that this might be the long-awaited breakthrough and some units were surprised by both the ease of their attack and the lack of German resistance.

During those first heady days the Gordons were represented by the following battalions: 1st Gordons attacking with the 3rd Division along the Arras–Cambrai road; 8/10th and 9th Gordons attacking with 15th (Scottish) Division in the centre on the left flank of the River Scarpe; 1/4th, 1/5th and 1/6th Gordons attacking on the left flank towards Bailleul with 51st (Highland) Division. During the attack of the 3rd Division, 1st Gordons had the heady sensation of sweeping forward rapidly to find the wire broken and the Germans offering limited resistance, but due to orders being delayed the battalion was forced to mount a second attack without the support of the 8th King's Regiment. Although 1st Gordons reached the objective the battalion found itself under enfilading machine-gun fire and was forced to retire, having sustained 276 casualties killed or wounded. Better fortune greeted 8/10th Gordons in the attack on Monchy-le-Preux. Despite coming under concentrated fire from a position known as 'Railway Triangle' the battalion managed to advance 1,000 yards beyond its objective. For the 51st (Highland) Division the opening rounds were equally successful, with all first objectives being taken. Throughout the battle 9th Gordons continued to serve in the essential pioneer role, building a light railway, marking tracks and clearing debris.

Three days later the tally for the Allies was encouraging. Vimy Ridge and Warncourt had been captured and thousands of Germans had been taken prisoner. Only in the centre at Roeux, on the north bank of the Scarpe, had the attack stalled. Thankfully the wintry conditions had also disappeared, but time was fast running out for the ever more exhausted assault battalions. Increased

German resistance and reinforcement meant higher casualties for the attacking forces: in the next phase of the battle there were to be no easy gains and the British attack soon faltered as the assault battalions came up against stronger German opposition and the British commander, General Sir Edmund Allenby, was forced to scale down the offensive. Some of the fiercest fighting was at Roeux, which had been captured briefly only for it to be retaken by the Germans. On 23 April a fresh assault on the straggling village and its associated chemical works was made by 51st (Highland) Division, and in common with other operations at this stage of the battle it was hurried and improvised. The preceding artillery barrage failed to unsettle the German defenders, who were in the process of rushing reinforcements into the village for an attack of their own. On the left $1/4^{th}$ Gordons ran into intensive machine-gun fire during its attack with $1/7^{th}$ Argylls and lost six officers and 48 soldiers killed and ten officers and 197 soldiers wounded. During 153 Brigade's attack $1/7^{th}$ Gordons was also pinned down by heavy machine-gun fire and lost 213 officers and soldiers killed, wounded or missing.

In the final phase of the battle 2nd Gordons enjoyed a measure of success on the Bullecourt Front, where over 100 German prisoners were taken. Roeux finally fell to the 4th Division but immediately came under fierce German counter-attack. Taken by surprise, $1/5^{th}$ Gordons recognised the seriousness of the situation and was largely responsible for driving the incoming Germans from the chemical works. In the final action of the battle, in mid-June, 1st Gordons succeeded in taking a hitherto impregnable objective known as Infantry Hill, which lay to the east of Monchy-le-Preux. Although the first day 'went without a hitch' (according to the diary of Lieutenant-Colonel R.A. Wolfe Murray), it was not the end of the fighting:

> Like a cat, however, the German always fought for his eyes and the six days following this success, when the Battn. was asked to hold on to what they had taken, were days and nights of terrific bombardment and the most tenacious counter attacks by the enemy. Casualties were terrific. There is one story of a Coy. being almost obliterated by the shell fire, for yards the dead could not be buried, being already buried by the trench blown in by shells. C.S.M. [Company Sergeant Major] Urquhart was only known to have been killed by his brother, A. L. Cpl. [Corporal], finding his legs and this gallant W.O. [Warrant Officer] was only one of many.

By the time that the fighting ended any hope of defeating the Germans at Arras had disappeared and the losses had multiplied. The British suffered around 159,000 casualties, a daily rate of 4,076 (higher than the Somme's 2,943), and the stuffing had been knocked out of many of the formations which had been involved in a month of hard fighting against a heavily reinforced enemy.

Later in the year, at the Third Battle of Ypres, also known as Passchendaele, all three Scottish divisions were again involved in the fighting to deepen the British-held Ypres Salient. The battle lasted four months and accounted for a quarter of a million casualties, 70,000 of them killed or drowned in the lagoons of mud which covered the battlefield. During the fighting on the first day, 31 July, 8/10th Gordons attacked German positions on the Frezenberg Ridge. Although they were accompanied by revolutionary armoured vehicles known as tanks, the issue was decided by close-quarter fighting with the bayonet. At the same time the Territorial battalions in 51st (Highland) Division crossed the Steenbeck River and succeeded in taking their objectives. The attack on the left was led by 1/7th Gordons, and during the attack of 153 Brigade the

British artillery barrage was carefully calibrated to fall in front of the advancing troops, leading one Gordon Highlander to exclaim: 'Mon, the barrage was that fine ye could have lighted your pipe at it!'

Late summer and autumn saw further successes, with the three Territorial battalions taking their objectives during the 51st (Highland) Division's attack on Poelcapelle. At one stage in the fighting a Gordons corporal came across an abandoned German tank on the Poelcapelle road and put its gun to good use by firing at the enemy. One of the main bugbears for the attacking battalions was the German defensive positions containing pill-boxes with heavy machine guns. As Wolfe Murray's diary makes clear, the capture of these fortified positions depended on a heavy bombardment and then nerves of steel to finish off the attack:

> The 'pill-box' was the Germans' very clever solution to the problem of how to defend a flooded boggy area. The mud of Passchendaele was terrific, every bit as bad as the Festubert area and the Germans built these pill-boxes to provide cover for their men just as we built the grouse butts in 1915. The pill-box was a hut made of reinforced concrete built above the level of the ground, size and thickness of concrete and design varying according to circumstances, but all had their entrances towards the German line, to our front and on either flank were only loop holes for the M.G.s [machine guns]. Our barrage would drive the Germans into these forts where they would lie doggo till the shells ceased to rain, it was then a race who got up first, the brave man with a stink bomb to throw in at either door or the German M.G.s; whoever was first won the day. The man who from outside the pill-box so closely followed our barrage as to be up in time and rushed up to throw the deadly bomb in, was a real hero.

In the last action of the battle 2nd Gordons was involved with 8th Devonshire in an attack west of Gheluvelt and both battalions were halted in their tracks by the heavy, cloying mud and the ferocity of the German enfilading machine-gun fire. The battalion's losses were four officers and 16 soldiers killed, and eight officers and 318 soldiers wounded or missing. In the following month the battalion was removed from the Western Front and sent to serve on the Italian front (see below). At the end of November the three Territorial battalions were involved in the Battle of Cambrai, which has the distinction of being the first battle in which tanks were used on a large scale – eight divisions with 324 tanks were involved in the main attack. The Germans were completely taken by surprise and by the end of the first day, 20 November, the British had advanced four miles on a six-mile front. As the regimental historian put it, the Gordons had a 'great day'; the 1/5th battalion cleared its objectives on the Hindenburg Line, taking 400 prisoners and losing only six killed and 56 wounded. But it was not all easy gains. As 1/6th Gordons waited to go into the attack on the Bapaume–Cambrai railway line the men were witnesses to a disaster when eleven tanks were put out of action near the village of Flesquières, and as the battalion moved forward it lost 60 casualties to German machine-gun positions which had not been destroyed. The battle ended inconclusively on 7 December. One of the lessons learned was that the infantry formations had to keep pace with the attacking tanks to have a chance of exploiting any breakthrough. The battle coincided with the collapse and surrender of Russia following the Bolshevik revolution, a move which allowed the Germans to transfer much-needed forces to the Western Front. The effect of that move would be felt the following year.

1918

The Western Front: 1st, 1/4th, 1/5th, 1/6th, 6/7th, 8/10th, 9th battalions

In March 1918 the German high command under General Erich von Ludendorff planned a major initiative to win the war before US forces were able to deploy in strength in Europe and at a time when the British and French armies had been badly weakened by the previous year's offensives. Conceived at a conference in Mons, held, ironically, on 11 November 1917, exactly a year before the war ended, the German plan took advantage of the fact that the Russian surrender had released substantial numbers of German troops which could be used on the Western Front against the British and French armies. Not only would this give Ludendorff a numerical advantage in the field, but many of the formations were tried and tested infantry regiments, Prussians, Guards and Swabians, representing the cream of the old German army. Ludendorff's strategy was brutally simple: his armies would drive a wedge between the two opposing armies, striking through the old Somme battlefield between Arras and La Fère before turning to destroy the British Third and Fifth Armies on the left of the Allied line. Three German armies would be used in the assault. The Second Army and the Seventeenth Army would take the offensive across the Somme battlefield before driving north to wrap up the British, while the Eighteenth Army provided flank support to the south in the St Quentin sector. Codenamed 'Michael' (Germany's patron saint), the offensive plan was adopted on 21 January 1918 and it called for a massive rolling 'hurricane' artillery barrage followed by a rapid and aggressive advance by the infantry which, in Ludendorff's words, would 'punch a hole' in the British defences and lay the foundations for defeating the enemy in Flanders. Strong-points would be bypassed to be wrapped up later by the mopping-up troops.

With the removal of the 2nd battalion to the Italian front and the later amalgamation of the 6th and 7th battalions to form 6/7th Gordons, the regiment was reduced to six battalions during the final decisive three months of the war. To meet a shortage of manpower each brigade was ordered to reduce its strength from four to three battalions, leaving each division with nine infantry battalions. The remaining three were used either as 'entrenching battalions' for drafting reserves or transferred to other divisions. This meant that 1/5th Gordons moved to the 61st Division on the St Quentin sector. At the onset of the German attack the Gordons' positions were as follows: 1/5th Gordons, north of St Quentin; 1/4th, 1/6th and 1/7th Gordons on the Bapaume–Cambrai road; 1st Gordons south-east of Arras, 8/10th and 9th Gordons to the north of Arras. First to feel the brunt of the German assault was 1/5th Gordons, under the command of Lieutenant-Colonel M.F. McTaggart, which was quickly overrun when the attack began on 21 March, and it ceased to exist as a unit. Only 30 survivors managed to make their way back to the rear area. Amongst the battalion's 560 casualties (killed, wounded or missing) was McTaggart who had served previously with 5th Royal Irish Lancers. Serving in the 61st Division's machine-gun battalion, Lieutenant A.E. Ker, 3rd Gordons, put up stout resistance and refused to surrender, holding out for three hours until his position was overwhelmed. For his gallantry he received the Victoria Cross (see Appendix).

Disaster also hit 1/7th Gordons, which formed 153 Brigade with 1/6th and 1/7th Black Watch, both of which had been badly depleted in the opening rounds of the German assault. As the Germans continued to press forward on 24 March the brigade was forced to withdraw towards Bapaume; the Gordons lost heavy casualties and their complement was eventually reduced to eight officers and 100 soldiers. In those fraught early days few believed that anything could stop the inexorable German assault but amidst the confusion of a battle which was the British Army's first defeat on the Western Front, Ludendorff's plan was beginning to unravel. By the beginning of April the Germans had advanced 20 miles along a 50-mile front, creating a huge bulge in the Allied line, and had pushed themselves to within five miles of Amiens. If this key city and railhead had fallen it would have been a disaster for the Allies. The French would have been forced back to defend Paris and the British would have been left with little option but to do the same to defend the Channel ports, and the war would have hung in the balance. However, despite the obvious dangers facing the Allies, the Germans had already shot their bolt by failing to concentrate the main thrust of their assault and dispersing the effort to take their targets. As the *Official History* puts it, 'These manifold objectives required more troops than Ludendorff had at his disposal.' While attacking along the Scarpe valley in front of Arras the Germans met determined resistance and took heavy casualties. Now involved in fighting an organised defensive battle, the 15th (Scottish Division) dug in and refused to budge; with accurate artillery fire to support them the fighting soldiers grew in confidence as they saw the enemy falling to their fire. At one stage during the battle two companies of 8/10th Gordons joined forces with 7th Camerons to defend the vital Neuville–Vitasse switch line on 28 March and held it against overwhelming odds, earning the praise of the divisional commander Major-General Sir George Carter-Campbell, who said 'in all sincerity' that 44th Brigade 'had saved Arras'.

The German attack also brought about a change in the Allies' command structure. Following an acrimonious conference at Doullens near Amiens on 26 March, it was agreed that General Foch would assume authority for directing the operations to defend Amiens with a joint British and French force, a change that would make him in effect the Allied generalissimo. The appointment of an overall commander came at the very moment when the initial German attack was faltering and the Michael offensive was finally called off on 5 April without Amiens coming under threat of attack. The German break-in battle had succeeded in capturing a large salient but it would prove difficult to hold and the expected breakthrough to split the Allies had failed to materialise. There had also been heavy German casualties – some 250,000 killed, missing or wounded – and morale within the assault formations had been shattered by their failure to produce a decisive blow in the so-called '*Kaiserschlacht*' (Kaiser's Battle) which was supposed to win the war. Even so, Ludendorff was not quite done with his offensive. Four days later, on 9 April, he launched Operation Georgette, a second attack aimed along a narrow front south of Armentières in the Ypres sector. An under-strength Portuguese division was brushed aside in the Aubers–Neuve–Chapelle sector, allowing the Germans to advance towards the defensive line of the rivers Lawe and Lys, which was eventually shored up by British XI Corps which included all the Gordons' Territorial battalions.

By that stage 1/7th Gordons numbered only 19 officers and 625 soldiers, many of whom were recent recruits. Nevertheless, it played a full role in the fighting south of the River Lys, where it formed a defensive position with 1/5th Seaforth and men of King Edward's Horse. Due to the rapidity with which the German attack unfolded, battalion War Diaries offer scant information about the course of the battle – an entry in the 1/5th battalion's War Diary concedes that there were 'many conflicting rumours' when 61st Division arrived to shore up the 51st (Highland) Division's line on 12 April. (Both 152 and 153 Brigades had taken heavy casualties and had been forced to retire the previous day.) The stand on the River Lys took the sting out of the German attack and although the enemy advanced beyond Merville and Bailleul to come within sight of Hazebrouck, the arrival of French reinforcements from

General Maistre's Tenth Army on 21 April stabilised the front. A week later Ludendorff called off the Georgette operation, bringing a degree of respite to the battered British First and Second Armies, which had taken the brunt of the attack in the Ypres sector. Casualties were high: the British lost 76,000, the French 35,000 and the Portuguese 6,000; on the German side there were 109,000 casualties. The Gordons' losses reflected the national figures: the $1/4^{th}$ battalion lost 200 officers and soldiers killed, wounded or missing, the $1/6^{th}$ battalion lost 358, the $1/7^{th}$ battalion 282 and the $8/10^{th}$ battalion 303. Although the losses in the $1/5^{th}$ battalion were not recorded, they cannot have been dissimilar. In May $8/10^{th}$ merged with the $1/5^{th}$ battalion to form 5th battalion The Gordon Highlanders in 44 Brigade, which formed part of 15th (Scottish) Division.

Following the failure of the attack on the British lines in the Somme and Ypres sectors Ludendorff turned his attention to the French armies along the Aisne. Once again the German assault forces achieved an initial success by breaching the opposition's defences and by 30 May they had reached the Marne, creating a salient 20 miles deep and 30 miles wide. Vigorous counter-attacks by French and newly arrived US forces frustrated the German advance and British forces were also involved when the newly formed XXII Corps, under Lieutenant General Sir Alexander Godley, was deployed in support of the French army in Champagne. Among its four divisions were 15th (Scottish) and 51st (Highland) and both of them took part in what became known as the Second Battle of the Marne, which finally halted the German advance in the middle of July. Five Gordons battalions were involved in the fighting ($1/4^{th}$, 5th, $1/6^{th}$, $1/7^{th}$ and 9th), the highest number of any regiment in the British Army. Much of the fighting took place in heavily wooded areas which made for difficulties in keeping direction while going forward, and during one attack on 22 July

French artillery fire fell short and caused casualties in the 1/6th battalion. (This was a common occurrence throughout the war and came to be known as 'friendly fire'.) By the end of the month the division had advanced four miles and taken large numbers of prisoners but this came at a cost: 1/6th Gordons lost 344 casualties killed, wounded or missing while the losses in 1/7th Gordons were 272.

On the western side of the salient 15th (Scottish) Division came under French command together with 34th Division. The main action took place against the village and chateau of Buzancy, both heavily defended objectives. The war had lasted four years yet the fighting spirit of most of the front-line soldiers seemed to be undiminished, as Alick Buchanan-Smith discovered while 5th Gordons waited to go into the attack:

> They were magnificent men in the bloom of youth. Again there was little or no personal anxiety in their faces or in their actions. In part perhaps this may have been because, by then, the war had become accepted almost as a way of life.
>
> I remember one of them vividly, partly because I had occasion to tick him off. He was a great strapping chield, bigger and broader than myself. His kilt still retained its pleats. Something stirred in me to ask him his age. 'Fifteen,' was his reply as he looked me straight in the eye. After Buzancy I never saw him again.

By afternoon the objective had been secured after some ferocious street and house-to-house fighting. The Second Battle of the Marne represented the last best chance for the Germans to win the war: for all that they had won large tracts of enemy ground, the salients had vulnerable flanks which were prone to counter-attack. The Germans had also taken huge casualties and for the survivors it was dispiriting to see that so little had been gained for so much effort. At the same time they were aware that the Americans were arriving in France at the rate of 300,000 a month and would soon produce a formidable opposition with fresh troops and a seemingly limitless supply of weapons and equipment. The beginning of the end came on 8 August, when Australian and Canadian forces attacked the German positions to the east of Amiens with a British and a French corps guarding the flank to the north and south. The attack achieved complete surprise and the Allies were able to advance eight miles in one day, taking over 12,000 German prisoners in the process. Writing in his memoirs the following year Ludendorff described 8 August as 'the black day of the German army in the history of this war. This was the worst experience I had to go through. Everything I had feared and of which I had so often given warning, had here, in one place, become a reality. Our war machine was no longer efficient.'

Following its adventures on the Marne 51st (Highland) Division returned to familiar territory on the Arras sector where the War Diary of 1/6th Gordons recorded a much-needed change in the environment:

> If left in peace, amenities of this place are considerable. The railway embankment, 70 feet high, affords complete protection for tiers or terraces of comfortable huts. Also a clean-flowing river and several lakes for bathing and even boating. The embankment gives cover to a large area in which free movement by day goes on.

Although the improvements were an indication of growing Allied strength the battalion was soon in action again, attacking Fampoux on 21 August. A few days later the same battalion watched in mild astonishment as Canadian forces moved forward inexorably behind a huge bombardment towards Monchy-le-Preux. A year earlier, during the Battle of Arras, it had been a seemingly impregnable obstacle. During the same attack 1/7th Gordons took Greenland Hill, another reminder of the previous year's fighting. Although the Germans put up stout resistance the Allies continued to go forward and 1st Gordons was part of 3rd Division's successful attack on Bapaume in the initial stages of the final push. Shortage of recruits and continuing casualties forced the 1/6th and 1/7th battalions to amalgamate at the beginning of October – the latter battalion consisted of three officers and 107 soldiers – and the resultant formation ended the war as 6/7th battalion The Gordon Highlanders.

The war now entered its final stages and during the final 100 days, as the period came to be known, the Gordons battalions were much altered from the 'originals' who had gone to war in 1914. The majority of the junior officers were recent arrivals and while they lacked nothing in vim and enthusiasm, their lack of experience often led to errors when things did not go according to plan. There was also a shortage of experienced non-commissioned officers but as the regimental historian noted: 'It was indeed a wonderful proof of the fortitude and endurance of British stock that after over four years of war, and a death roll for the British Isles only and the Army alone now approaching 700,000, it was still capable of winning so great a victory.' All along the front line the Allies made steady progress as the weakened German forces began pulling back towards their homeland. As 1st Gordons pushed towards Le Quesnoy the lead units of 3rd Division encountered a new menace: mustard gas, which was used increasingly indiscriminately. As Sergeant H.E. May wrote in a memoir for the anthology *Everyman at War*, the effects were beyond belief:

> A working party was required one night to dig a cable trench. It is impossible to do navvies' work in a box respirator and the party mainly worked without. A deluge of gas shells. Eyes swollen and red; throats parched; flesh inflamed and almost raw where the mustard variety had burned it – a serious disadvantage to a kilt . . . In the garden at the billet lying about the grass were close on a hundred men, denuded of their clothing, who lay about and writhed in veriest agony. The worst gas cases. With the passing of a few hours huge blisters were raised by the mustard gas. One man had a blister that reached from his neck to the bottom of his spine and extended the whole width of his back. In their agony they were retching horribly; straining till they sank exhausted, and then suddenly vomiting a long, green, streamer-like substance. And they were nearly all blind.

May had started off in the Cameron Highlanders before transferring to the Gordons in May 1917; with his new regiment he was awarded the Military Medal in October 1918. During those final weeks of the war 1/4th, 5th and 6/7th Gordons were in constant action during the advance to the River Selle. Casualties continued to be high – in the action against Famars at the end of October 1/4th Gordons lost 210 casualties, the majority wounded or missing. At long last the Armistice arrived on 11 November, but there was little overt rejoicing. The men of 6/7th Gordons lit a bonfire but an entry in the War Diary of the 1/4th battalion says it all: 'Such a day is difficult to realise.'

1917–18
Italy: 2nd battalion

Italy had started the First World War as ostensible allies of Germany and Austria-Hungary. Through the Triple Alliance of 1882 (renewed in 1906) it was bound to both countries, but using diplomatic sleight of hand it had managed to evade responsibility for meeting its conditions by claiming that they only applied to a defensive war. In any case the country's armed forces were in no position to take any serious initiative: its army could make no intervention in France and Flanders and its Mediterranean fleet was outgunned by the British and French navies. Knowing that Italy retained territorial ambitions in Tyrol and Slovenia, which had been lost in the Austro–Italian War of 1866, the British spent a good deal of diplomatic effort in wooing Italy with promises of territorial aggrandisement should it throw in its lot with the Allies. In vain did the Germans counter by promising to return the territory which had been annexed by Vienna. Encouraged by King Victor Emmanuel III, the Italian government signed the secret Treaty of London on 26 April 1915, committing Italy to joining Britain, France and Russia in return for the territory held by Austria-Hungary and the Dodecanese islands in the eastern Mediterranean which had been lost to Turkey in 1912. A month later Italy declared war on Austria-Hungary and put its 875,000 soldiers on a war footing.

From the outset the Italians were at a serious disadvantage. Not only was the army mostly composed of reservists but it was chronically short of equipment. One example will suffice to illustrate many of its shortcomings: its 36 infantry divisions and two Alpine army groups possessed only 600 machine guns. On top of that lack of materiel, the army's senior commanders had to grapple with an unpromising strategic situation. Italy shared a mountainous frontier with Austria-Hungary from the Tyrol in the west to the Julian Alps in the east, a precipitous region 375 miles in length which contained some of the highest mountains in Europe. At the western extremity lay the Trentino with its high mountain passes, and in the east the valley of the River Isonzo gave way to the high plateaux of the Bainsazza and the Carso, an area which the *Official History* described as a 'howling wilderness of stones sharp as knives'. Worse, the Austro-Hungarian army had seized the initiative by seizing the high ground, forcing the Italians to remain on the defensive in the Trentino sector and limiting its offensive operations on the Isonzo front.

Under the overall command of General Luigi Cadorna, soon to become infamous as a martinet with a profligate disregard for men's lives, the Italian army opened its account on the Isonzo, using its skilled Alpine troops in the vanguard. Cadorna hoped that a rapid advance would surprise the enemy and the weight of the attack would take his army into enemy territory. It did not turn out that way. Most of the Austro-Hungarian regiments were militia formations but they fought with great doggedness, and despite four Italian offensives the year ended with the Isonzo front stabilised and with 121,118 Italian casualties (killed or wounded). Coupled with the German/Austro-Hungarian victory over the Russians at Gorlice-Tarnow that same year, the balance of power shifted on the eastern and Alpine fronts allowing Germany to concentrate more of its efforts on the Western Front in 1916. Field Marshal Conrad von Hötzendorf, the Austro-Hungarian Chief of Staff, used this advantage to good effect by launching an assault on the Trentino front aimed at the lagoons at Venice. Following a massive artillery bombardment the Austro-Hungarian army went into the attack on 15 May and managed to advance 10 miles before Cadorna's forces managed to regroup. Having stemmed the enemy assault the Italians returned to the Isonzo front, launching four attacks before the year came to an end. None of these brought any strategic result other than to tie up Austro-Hungarian forces which might otherwise have been employed on the Russian front.

The following year brought the disaster at Caporetto which undid all the previous efforts and led to Italian demands for rapid reinforcement by the Allies. Fought between 24 October and 12

November 1917 on the Trentino front, it followed yet another unsuccessful Italian offensive on the Isonzo sector and resulted in huge Italian losses – 30,000 casualties (killed or wounded) and 250,000 taken prisoner. This was followed by an equally disastrous slump in morale, due not least to Cadorna's disciplinary methods and his indifference to his soldiers' suffering, which finally led to his sacking and replacement by General Armando Diaz. Five British and six French infantry divisions were despatched to the Italian front, which had been stabilised on the River Piave to the north-east of Venice. Amongst the formations sent to join XIV Corps under the command of Lieutenant-General Lord Cavan was 7th Division, which included 2nd Gordons. The British forces began arriving in December 1917 and initially the 7th Division was held in reserve, during which time, according to the regimental historian, 2nd Gordons 'could not have found a quieter front'. At the end of February came news that the 7th Division was to return to France but the order was reversed and 2nd Gordons remained on the Italian front until the end of the war.

It was not until the end of April that the battalion, under the command of Lieutenant-Colonel F.M. Crichton Maitland, moved to the Montello sector on the left of the Allied line, where the high Asiago Plateau provided extreme weather conditions with snow and low temperatures. An outbreak of influenza led to the battalion being withdrawn to the plains and it was not until October that the British forces were in serious action, when they took part in an offensive along the Piave in an attempt to split the Austro-Hungarian forces. Launched on 23 October, it involved the difficult crossing of the River Piave, which was achieved with the help of Italian boatmen and by capturing an island (Grave di Papadopoli) before building pontoon bridges to complete the crossing. Having secured the island 2nd Gordons led the assault, attacking under heavy Austro-Hungarian artillery fire. At one point it seemed that the attack might falter but the advance enemy positions were held by weak Hungarian troops who, according to the regimental historian, 'had not fixed their bayonets and had no stomach for fighting Highlanders at close quarters'. During the fighting, which became known as the Battle of Vittorio Veneto, 2nd Gordons lost three officers and 11 soldiers killed and three officers and 57 soldiers wounded or missing.

The advance was continued to the rivers Montecano and Livenza and during the operation the battalion was presented with scenes of a rapid collapse in enemy morale – dead horses, abandoned equipment and looted shops in the towns through which the fleeing Austro-Hungarian army had passed. On 4 November an armistice came into being and for 2nd Gordons the war ended in the Trissino area. It was not until 23 December that demobilisation began, a process that was already in hand on the Western Front.

For 1st Gordons there was the privilege of marching into Germany to form the army of occupation known as the British Army of the Rhine. Later, the battalion would be joined by 1/4th and 5th Gordons. For the other Territorial and New Army battalions there was a reduction to cadre strength before amalgamation for the former and disbandment for the latter. It was not until June 1919 that the process was finally completed. This was a difficult and contentious time, with some men, such as miners and other essential workers, being given priority, but the Gordons battalions escaped the unrest which unsettled many regiments in 1919. As the regimental historian put it: 'It would be unjust to many other good regiments to say that the Gordons' discipline was outstanding. Let us put it that it need not fear comparison with the best.'

EIGHT

The Second World War: 1939–42

Following the Armistice in November 1918 the slow business of disbanding the huge volunteer wartime army began. All the service battalions raised for the New Armies were disbanded and there was also a gradual contraction in the size of the Territorial battalions. For the Gordons this meant that the 8th, 9th, 10th and 11th battalions marched into history while the 5th and 7th battalions were amalgamated in 1934 to form 5/7th Gordons (the 4th and 6th battalions remained unscathed). There was also disbandment for one of the lesser-known wartime formations, the 1st Garrison Battalion Gordon Highlanders, which had been formed in 1916 and was made up of men unfit for active service. It served at Rawalpindi in India until January 1920, when it was brought home and disbanded. The London Scottish continued its association with the regiment and in 1937 was redesignated The London Scottish, Gordon Highlanders. For the two regular battalions there were differing experiences in the immediate post-war period. As a result of the civil wars in Ireland (known variously as the Anglo-Irish

War or War of Independence) which preceded independence in 1921 both the 1st and the 2nd battalions were stationed there as part of the security forces backing the Royal Irish Constabulary. The 1st battalion served in Ireland between October 1919 and January 1920 and the 2nd served first in 1919 and again in 1921. It was a squalid little conflict with murders and revenge killings carried out by both sides, the Irish Republican Army (IRA) as well as the security forces. 'The whole country runs with blood,' ran a leader in the *Irish Times* on 20 April 1921. 'Unless it is stopped and stopped soon every prospect of political settlement and material prosperity will perish and our children will inherit a wilderness.' The commander-in-chief at the time was General Sir Nevil Macready, who had served with 1st Gordons at Tel-el-Kebir and was himself an Irishman. It was not until the end of 1921 that a political solution was imposed on the country and its warring factions, but the decision to keep the six Ulster counties separate from the Irish Free State was to cause equally vexing problems later in the century.

A different and more exotic posting awaited 1st Gordons. The conclusion of hostilities had not just left Europe in chaos, the Middle East was also in a state of turmoil following the break-up of the Ottoman Empire and the carve-up of its provinces amongst Britain, France, Greece and Italy. This was followed by rioting in Cairo and outbreaks of disorder in Palestine, Transjordan (present-day Jordan) and in 1921 in Iraq. There was also trouble in Constantinople, where the Turkish nationalists had won a general election in 1919 and had immediately created a National Pact calling for the creation of an independent Turkish nation-state. The emergence of the nationalists under Mustafa Kemal (better known as Kemal Atatürk) led to confrontation with the Allies and it soon became clear that they did not possess sufficient forces to contain the problem. Following a series of French defeats in Cilicia, bordering Syria, Britain led an Allied occupation force which moved to Constantinople in mid-March 1920, declared martial law and dissolved the Chamber of Deputies. Kemal responded by setting up a Grand National Assembly in Angora and the stage was set for a bitter internecine war which quickly descended into anarchy, with rival warlords settling old scores and making opportunist bids to strengthen their positions.

Following a short spell in Catterick, 1st Gordons received orders in March 1920 to join the Army of the Black Sea, the British intervention force which was deployed in Constantinople to deal with the Kemalist rebellion. In common with all counter-insurgency conflicts it was a time-consuming operation which required great patience, not least when the battalion was operating with Greek troops, most of whom were illiterate. (As part of the Allied carve-up Smyrna had been awarded to the Greeks whose prime minister, Eleutherios Venizelos, had committed troops to assist the Army of the Black Sea.) Eventually Britain decided to offer concessions to Kemal, who was being wooed by Bolshevik Russia, and a slackening in local tensions allowed the battalion to be withdrawn to Malta in November 1921. It was, however, only a respite: following Kemal's defeat of the Greeks in the summer of 1922 1st Gordons was rushed to the Dardanelles, where British forces acted as a buffer between the rival forces at Chanak (present day Canakkale) on the Asiatic side. The crisis subsided in 1923, allowing the Gordons to return to Malta during the summer.

On New Year's Day 1924 1st Gordons left for a posting in India which lasted until 1934, when the battalion moved to Haifa in Palestine to take part in internal security duties as tensions increased between the Arab and Jewish populations. Regimental records at this time show that 83 per cent of the battalion's complement were Scots, the majority from Aberdeen and the north-east. As the home battalion 2nd Gordons spent the period 1921–34 in Scotland and

Ireland, but it would soon be on the move again. By the end of the 1930s it was obvious to many that once more the world was heading towards war. In Germany the Nazis had come to power under Adolf Hitler and their presumptuous territorial claims were soon trying the patience of the rest of Europe. In 1938 Prime Minister Neville Chamberlain seemed to have bought 'peace in our time' following his negotiations with Hitler in Munich, which gave the Germans a free hand in the Sudetenland and subsequently in Bohemia and Moravia. However, it proved to be the calm before the storm. Having signed a peace pact with the Soviet Union Hitler then felt free to invade Poland at the beginning of September 1939. Chamberlain, who would be replaced as prime minister by Winston Churchill the following year, had no option but to declare war – Britain and Poland were bound by treaty – but the country's armed forces were hardly in a fit condition to fight a modern war. The British Army could put together only four divisions as an expeditionary force for Europe, six infantry and one armoured division in the Middle East, a field division and a brigade in India, two brigades in Malaya and a modest scattering of imperial garrisons elsewhere. Years of neglect and tolerance of old-fashioned equipment meant that the army was ill-prepared to meet the modern German forces in battle and British industry was not geared up to make good those deficiencies. Once again in the nation's history it seemed that Britain was going to war with the equipment and mentality of previous conflicts. Events in Poland quickly showed that Germany was a ruthless and powerful enemy whose Blitzkrieg tactics allowed it to sweep aside lesser opposition: using armour and air power the Germans swept into the country, which fell within 18 days of the invasion allowing Hitler to turn his attention to defeating France.

To bolster the French the British government deployed a British Expeditionary Force (BEF), which included Regular and

Territorial battalions of The Gordon Highlanders. In 1939 1st Gordons had already returned from Palestine and was based at Aldershot, where it formed 2 Brigade with 1st Loyal Regiment and 2nd North Staffordshire Regiment in the 1st Division commanded by Major-General the Hon. H.R.L.G. Alexander, later Field Marshal Earl Alexander of Tunis. The other Gordons committed to the BEF were the 5th and 6th battalions, which served in the 51st (Highland) Division and 4th Gordons, which had been converted to a machine-gun battalion as General Headquarters troops. (Owing to increasing numbers of recruits in 1939 the amalgamation of 5th and 7th battalions was ended, but it was restored a year later.) Before crossing over to France the Gordons and the other Highland regiments received an order from the War Office that kilts were not to be worn in France. In response Lieutenant-Colonel Alick Buchanan-Smith, commanding 5th Gordons, arranged a special parade before embarkation when a Gordons kilt was ceremoniously burned on the square at Bordon in Hampshire.

During the course of the war the regiment underwent several changes. As we shall see, the 1st and 2nd battalions were destined to go into enemy captivity during the opening rounds of the war against Germany and Japan and had to be reconstituted. On returning from Dunkirk the 4th battalion experienced another transformation, to become 92nd Anti-Tank Regiment, Royal Artillery. The 8th and 9th battalions were raised as part of the expansion of the Territorial Army in 1939 and served respectively as 100th Anti-Tank Regiment, Royal Artillery and 116th Regiment Royal Armoured Corps. A home defence unit was formed in 1936 as 10th (Home Defence) Battalion, becoming 30th Gordons in 1941. The London Scottish produced three battalions – the 1st battalion served in the Middle East and Italy while the 3rd battalion served as 97th Anti-Aircraft regiment, Royal Artillery.

FRANCE AND FLANDERS

1st (old), 4th, 5th, 6th battalions

The first sign of imminent hostilities was the return of the reservists to the 1st battalion at Aldershot and the battalion crossed over to Cherbourg and proceeded to 1st Division's assembly area south-east of Lille where the BEF began creating defensive systems at Templeuve and Cysoing. The regular battalion was followed by 4th Gordons which crossed over to France at the end of October and moved to Roubaix under the general command of 4th Division in II Corps. By then the 51st (Highland) Division had also moved south in preparation for deployment in France. With it went the 5th and 6th battalions which formed 153 Brigade along with 4th Black Watch under the command of Brigadier G.T. Burney, a distinguished Gordon Highlander. The division was under the command of Major-General Victor Fortune and it was the first Territorial division to cross over to France, a fact which was acknowledged in March 1940, when each brigade was strengthened by exchanging one of its Territorial battalions for a Regular battalion. As a result 1st Gordons took the place of 6th Gordons in 153 Brigade, with the latter taking the former's place in 2 Brigade of the 1st Division.

This was the period which came to be known as 'the phoney war' and the lull in hostilities allowed the battalions to strike up friendships with the local population and units of the French army, rekindling memories of the historic 'Auld Alliance' between France and Scotland. All that came to an end on 10 May, when Hitler's forces attacked Holland and Belgium and the fighting on the Western Front began in earnest with the BEF moving into Belgium to take up prearranged positions along the River Dyle. The first of the battalions to go into action was 6th Gordons, which came under machine-gun fire from enemy aircraft on 14 May and two days later had its first experience of artillery bombardment, during which one officer and two soldiers were killed and five others were wounded. This was followed by a defensive action involving 4th Gordons north of Brussels. When the Gordons passed through the Belgian capital they were astonished to see signs of normality, with tramcars running and people going about their business as if there were no war. However, this unreal period was also remembered for the huge numbers of refugees on the roads. As the regimental history records, 'There seemed to be little attempt at traffic control and the frequent jams and delays tried the tempers of everyone.' By then Field Marshal Lord Gort, the BEF's commander-in-chief, had decided to withdraw in stages to the River Escaut.

The men of the BEF passed through a countryside rich with names that were redolent of the fighting in Flanders during the century's earlier conflict – Tournai, Armentières, Bailleul and Lille. At one point 4th and 6th Gordons found themselves fighting within two miles of each other on the line of the Escaut. This was a chaotic period for the British forces and although both Gordon battalions were in continuous contact with the enemy they were also involved in a desperate rearguard action which quickly degenerated into a full-scale retreat. By then the Germans had swept aside the French Ninth Army and were heading rapidly towards the Somme. Faced with the possibility of encirclement, and knowing that his lines of communication to the Channel were no longer secure, Gort prepared plans to pull the BEF back towards the port of Dunkirk. As the month drew to a close 6th Gordons had reached Poperinghe, where the men were ordered to dump all unnecessary equipment and to disable their lorries and carriers before heading for the Dunkirk perimeter. Under cover of dark the battalion reached the beaches on 1 June to begin the last stage of the evacuation back to England. The last unit to leave was the anti-tank company commanded by Major L.G. Murray. Also fighting its way back to the coast was 4th Gordons, which took part in a spirited defensive action along the canal between Comines and Ypres. Under fierce

German aerial bombardment the battalion reached the Dunkirk beaches on the morning of 1 June, when it received orders to make a last stand, should it become necessary. That turned out not to be the case and the battalion was evacuated the following day.

A different fate awaited the regiment's two other battalions. While the 6th battalion was involved in the great escape at Dunkirk on 1 June the 1st and 5th battalions were deployed with the rest of the 51st (Highland) Division along a defensive line to the south-west of Abbeville near the mouth of the River Somme. Sixty miles away to the south-west lay the small port of St Valéry-en-Caux, with the road via Dieppe forming a southern boundary, and it was within that area that the division would make its last stand. The 51st (Highland) Division had started the war under French command in the Saar region, where its armoured support was provided by the Mark VIb light tanks of the Lothian and Borders Horse, a yeomanry regiment, but following the initial German onslaught it had been compelled to withdraw towards the fortified positions in the French Maginot Line. The speed of the German Army's armoured assault meant that the division was cut off from the rest of the BEF and its fortunes were now tied firmly to the French Third Army under the command of General Besson.

During the switch from the Saar front the Gordons lost a number of casualties and these were keenly felt in the 5th battalion, where most of the soldiers came from the same locality. The strengths and weaknesses in the Territorial system are symbolised by the commanding officer, Lieutenant-Colonel Alick Buchanan-Smith, who had served in the regiment during the First World War. Like his father, who was principal of Aberdeen University, he was an academic in civilian life and he felt a strong emotional attachment to his men. His memories of May 1940 are indicative of the tensions felt by the part-time soldiers and his paternal attitude towards them during that difficult time: 'I remember being very much struck by the seriousness in their [soldiers'] faces and how they put their confidence in the officers. I wondered how many would ever again possess those boyish faces.' At the Petit Wolscher Wood on 13 May one casualty in the 5th battalion was 2nd Lieutenant Scott Raeburn, a well-liked officer whose brother George served as mortar officer in the same battalion. (They were one of three pairs of brothers in 5th Gordons.) During the same action Buchanan-Smith had a sharp disagreement with Burney over sending reinforcements to relieve 4th Black Watch in the woods south of Remeling and was later replaced on medical grounds (he was suffering from shingles) by his second-in-command, Major Rupert Christie, a Regular officer.

During this difficult period it became clear to the British high command that some elements in the French army were considering suing for peace. As these included the commander-in-chief General Maxime Weygande and Marshal Philippe Pétain, the renowned commander of the First World War, the threat had to be taken seriously. Churchill was determined to keep France in the war at all costs and that necessity was to play a part in determining the fate of Fortune's division. If the French were to sue for an armistice, as had been threatened, it would allow their powerful navy to fall into German hands and make an invasion of Britain more likely. At the same time, Churchill wanted to withdraw the bulk of the BEF through Dunkirk, even though that decision gave the impression to the French that their allies were pulling out and leaving them to their fate. As the 51st (Highland) Division continued to move further back into Flanders the political thinking in London was to have a decisive effect on what happened to them in the days ahead. Basically, Churchill's policy was to keep the 51st (Highland) Division in France as a means of keeping up pressure on the French to stay in the war at a time when defeatism was in the air. The War Diary of 1st Gordons describes a deserted landscape east of Tours, with cows un-milked and livestock wandering at will.

On 4 June the division supported a French attack made by the remnants of the French armoured and artillery forces along the Mareuil ridge to the south of Abbeville, its aim being control of the Somme crossings, but although the French fought with great determination, they were outnumbered and outgunned. This was the last full-scale Allied attack of 1940, but whatever its outcome the 51st (Highland) Division was now on its own in France, together with the remnants of the 1st Armoured Division and other assorted units. The following day, the Germans launched a fresh offensive along the line between the Somme and the Aisne and the overwhelming power of their offensive sealed the division's fate as it withdrew to the coast. It was a time of desperate fighting and confusion, when men were exhausted both by the need to retreat and to fight a rampant enemy. To the end Fortune hoped to pull his division out of Le Havre but after almost two weeks of hard fighting, on 12 June he was forced to surrender to his opponents, the German 7th Panzer Division led by General Erwin Rommel. In a last gesture of defiance 5th Gordons was ordered to make one final effort to clear the cliff-top positions outside the town, but this was forestalled when the French started surrendering in the face of a German tank attack. For one young officer, 2nd Lieutenant Donald Ritchie, who had earlier won the Military Cross, it was a harrowing moment which was recorded in Saul David's history of the action at St Valéry-en-Caux:

> I was completely overcome by emotion. Tears rolled down my cheeks. I was keyed up to attack this bloody ridge and then the reversal. I'll never forget Platoon Sergeant Herbie Forsyth giving me a wallop on the back and a bottle of brandy to swig from and saying, 'It's not your fault, sir.' It was a terrible thing and we were completely unprepared.

More than 10,000 British troops went into captivity following the surrender, and for the Gordons the surrender meant the loss of their 1st and 5th battalions, but every Highland regiment was also affected and in the Highland areas of Scotland there were scarcely any families who were unaffected by the loss of the division. Later, like a phoenix, a new 51st (Highland) Division would come into being, made up of replacement battalions which took the battalion numbers of those that had been lost at St Valéry. Those were desperate days, yet as the weeks and months wore on there was the heartening news that substantial numbers had managed to escape. Others tried to escape from captivity and some managed, one of the most notable being Lieutenant Peter de Winton, 1st Gordons, who escaped from Poland and ended up fighting with the Polish resistance. For the rest, the war meant five long years in camps in Germany and Poland where the men were given agricultural work or laboured in coal mines, a dispiriting fate for Highland soldiers who had gone to war in high expectation of repeating the feats of their fathers' generation two decades earlier.

THE FAR EAST

2nd battalion (old)

Following a deployment in Gibraltar, in March 1937 the 2nd battalion was ordered east to Singapore, where the men moved into Selerang Barracks at Changi. Malaya (present-day Malaysia) was a valuable asset as it produced almost 40 per cent of the world's rubber and 58 per cent of the world's tin, but at the time there was a good deal of complacency about the defence of this strategically important colony and the huge naval base at Singapore: the garrison consisted of three British battalions, a Malay battalion and an Indian battalion on Penang Island. The prevailing view, put by Winston Churchill in a paper to the Cabinet while he was First Lord of the Admiralty in December 1939, was that Singapore was an impregnable fortress and that it could only be reduced by a siege involving 50,000 men. As such, any potential enemy – probably Japan – would find it a difficult target to take:

> As Singapore is as far away from Japan as Southampton is from New York, the operation of moving a Japanese army with all its troop-ships and maintaining it with men and munitions during a siege would be forlorn. Moreover such a siege, which would last at least four or five months, would be liable to be interrupted, if at any time Britain chose to send a superior fleet to the scene . . . It is not considered possible that the Japanese, who are a prudent people and reserve their strength for the command of the Yellow Sea and China, in which they are fully occupied, would embark on such a mad enterprise.

Events were to prove Churchill tragically wrong. On Sunday 7 December 1941 Japan entered the war with its infamous pre-emptive air strike on the US Pacific Fleet's base at Pearl Harbor in Hawaii. This was followed in quick succession by further Japanese attacks on the islands of Guam, Wake and Midway while the Japanese Second Fleet escorted General Tomoyoku Yamashita's Twenty-Fifth Army to attack the north-west coast of the Malay peninsula. At the same time, three Japanese divisions prepared to invade the British colony of Hong Kong in southern China, a vital port and trading centre which had been in British hands since 1842. However, it was the collapse of Malaya and the surrender of Singapore on 15 February 1942 which caused the biggest dent to British pride and prestige in the region. Coupled with the concurrent invasion of Burma, the Japanese were suddenly in a position to threaten British interests in India, the 'jewel in the crown' of the country's imperial holdings.

This was to be one of the biggest disasters for the Allies at any stage in the war. Too late, the garrisons in Malaya and Singapore had been reinforced, but mostly by raw and untried troops. In 1941 command had been assumed by Lieutenant-General Arthur Percival, who had divided the island into three sectors: the southern was held by two Malay and one Straits Settlement Volunteer brigades, the western by 8th Australian Division and 44 Indian Infantry Brigade and the north by 9th and 11th Indian Divisions. Shortly before the Japanese attack 18th British Division arrived, but it took little part in the fighting. There was virtually no air cover and most of it was provided by obsolescent aircraft. Some idea of the problems facing 2nd Gordons can be found in an order forbidding them from using their bren carriers for more than 150 miles a month in case the tracks wore out. The battalion was also obliged to send drafts back to Britain and the make-up of the battalion was in a state of constant flux. Nonetheless, it retained its discipline and professionalism under trying conditions and it would need all that and more when it finally went into action in the defensive positions which had been rapidly organised in Johore to the north.

The story of the fall of Singapore is soon told. On 8 February the Japanese started crossing from Johore into the territory and within three days had gained a substantial foothold as Percival's forces moved back into the perimeter. Faced by tanks and bombed from the air, 2nd Gordons attempted a counter-attack at Bukit Timah village near the Alexandra Barracks but time was running out. On Friday, 13 February, the Japanese intensified their attacks by shelling the civilian areas and causing great damage, creating large numbers of casualties. By then it had become clear to Percival that further resistance was futile: water supplies were running low and a defensive battle would only cause unacceptable numbers of civilian casualties. An offensive operation might have brought results but this was rejected by his senior commanders. On 15 February, following a final conference, the fateful decision was taken to surrender and as a result 2nd Gordons, together with 14,000 Australian, 16,000 British and 32,000 Indian troops went into captivity. Ahead lay long and painful years of slave labour on the Burma–Siam railway where the sick rate and death rate quickly soared although, with a touch of regimental pride, the Gordons' war historian noted that 'in the Highlander abode a tough pride – almost arrogance – which no indignity devised by an Asiatic could subdue'. During the Singapore operations and the years in captivity the battalion lost 380 officers and men and their sacrifice is remembered on a memorial plaque in the Presbyterian Church in Singapore.

NORTH AFRICA

1st (new), 5/7th, 6th battalions

Following the loss of the original 51st (Highland) Division at St Valéry, a new 51st (Highland) Division was re-formed out of another equally distinguished Scottish formation, the 9th (Scottish) Division, which had come into being during the First World War as part of Kitchener's New Army. It was renumbered as the 51st and given the famous HD divisional sign and quickly started building up its own *esprit de corps* with the divisional headquarters in Rothes, Banffshire under the command of Major-General Neil Ritchie, Black Watch. The new division's Gordons contingent consisted of the re-formed 1st battalion (Lieutenant-Colonel K.G. O'Morchoe followed by Lieutenant-Colonel G.E. Malcolm) and the newly reamalgamated 5/7th battalion (Lieutenant-Colonel H.W.B. Saunders). Both were brigaded in 153 Brigade with 5th Black Watch. The 2nd battalion was also reconstituted, mainly from the 11th battalion which itself had its origins in the 50th Holding Battalion, which had been raised for training purposes in May 1940. At the time of the change the

11th battalion was engaged on home defence duties on Orkney but in September 1943, as 2nd Gordons, the battalion moved south to Yorkshire to join the 15th (Scottish) Division.

At the end of March 1942 the new Highland Division, now under the command of Major-General Douglas Wimberley, moved to Aldershot where it first encountered General Bernard Montgomery, GOC South-East Command, a soldier with whom the Highlanders would be closely associated for the rest of the war. Later that summer, in the middle of June, the entire division set sail from various ports bound for North Africa, a long and bruising voyage round the Cape of Good Hope which lasted 59 days and for most of the men felt even longer. Had it not been for a stop at Cape Town, where there was a chance for some shore leave and some splendid entertainment from the local community it could have been a depressing experience.

Having arrived in Egypt the division started training for desert warfare, getting used to the heat and dust and hardening themselves for the shock of battle. This was a difficult period for the British forces in the country. In June the British Eighth Army had fallen back from Tobruk, which fell into enemy hands following a German and Italian offensive led by General Erwin Rommel; Cairo was under threat and it seemed inevitable that another enemy assault would lead to the collapse of British power in North Africa. Morale was low and defeat seemed inevitable. At that point Churchill decided to change the command structure by appointing Montgomery to take over the Eighth Army. It proved to be an inspired choice and the tempo of training quickly increased to adapt the soldiers to the very different conditions of the desert.

Montgomery showed a sure touch in directing his first battle – the Battle of Alamein – which began on 23 October and turned out to be the first decisive British land victory of the war. Not only did he bring scrupulous planning to the preparations, but he also instilled a belief in the Eighth Army that they had the training and the equipment to defeat an enemy which was thought unbeatable. It was also a set-piece battle similar to the kind that had been fought in the latter stages of the First World War, with soldiers advancing under a heavy barrage and battalions leap-frogging forward to take their objectives. For the attack of the 51st (Highland) Division the intention was to secure 7,000 yards of desert, fighting across minefields and barbed wire, with the division advancing in six channels towards its objectives. Thus 1st Gordons and 5th Black Watch advanced on the right towards Montrose, Arbroath and Forfar (Green Line) before pushing on to Turiff (Red Line), then on to Kintore, Dufftown and Braemar (Black Line) with Aberdeen (Blue Line) being the final objective. For 5/7th Gordons in the next channel the objectives were Elgin and Cruden (Green Line), Inch (Red Line), Strichen and Stanley (Black Line) and Ballater (Blue Line). At 9.40 p.m. a huge artillery barrage opened up as hundreds of guns fired towards the German lines. As remembered by Lieutenant Felix Barker in his account of 5/7th Gordons, it was a moment which none would forget:

> Each man could see the white St Andrew's Cross on the back of the man in front of him. And as they moved forward they could not help feeling that the whole thing was rather fantastic. It was like no battle they had ever heard of, or could have imagined, in the wildest flight of imagination. Magazines were filled because it seemed out of the question to go into a major attack without rounds in the rifles, but many a man never fired a shot all that terrible night. Bayonets gleamed in the moonlight, but they were fixed as a token gesture, not so much to be used as to give confidence. A few men started at the high port with text-book punctilio but most had slung their rifles before long.

The attacking force moved off shortly after 10.00 p.m., each battalion being guided by a navigation officer watching his compass and counting his paces to ensure accuracy. All the first objectives were quickly taken, with the follow-up forces passing through the first wave; by dawn the following day the second objectives had also been taken and the battle moved into its next phase, which Montgomery promised would be a 'dog-fight'. All the time shelling continued on either side and tank battles raged as British Sherman tanks engaged the enemy lines. The battle continued for over a week and every Gordon Highlander experienced the common lot of the 51st (Highland) Division – of being under constant mortar- and shell-fire and of being pinned down by artillery as the forward formations attempted to make the final breakthrough. However, the speed and aggression of the Allied assault had broken the enemy's will to resist and on 3 November came the joyous confirmation from the BBC that there had been 'a great victory in North Africa'. That same day Operation Supercharge was put into effect as British, Indian and New Zealand forces fought their way out of the German lines of barbed wire and minefields to allow the armoured forces to begin the chase after the now retreating German and Italian forces. Hidden minefields were the main problem and both the Gordons battalions lost casualties during the pursuit phase but the fighting in North Africa was nearing its triumphant conclusion. Soon Montgomery's advancing men were passing well-known names which had become familiar to the Allies during the years of attack and retreat – Benghazi, Sidi Barrani, El Agheila, El Adem, Mersa Brega – as they raced towards the strategically important goal of the port of Tripoli, which fell at the end of January 1943. The first formation into the place was 1st Gordons, but the war diarist of 5/7th Gordons was not overly impressed by what the battalion found when it arrived: 'Tripoli is not much: a few fly-blown shops selling razor-blades and soap, and a moderately filthy Arab quarter.'

The next stage was the advance to Tunis to link up with the First Army, which was approaching to rendezvous with the Eighth Army. (A joint British and US army had landed in Morocco and Algiers at the beginning of November 1942, as part of Operation Torch. One of its more successful commanders was Lieutenant-General George Smith Patton, whose name would be heard of again.) Amongst those serving in the 1st British Division was 6th Gordons, which had landed in Algiers on 9 March 1943 as part of the reinforcements, after sailing from the Clyde. During the journey the ship carrying the battalion's vehicles and stores had been attacked and sunk, which meant that essential weapons such as mortars were missing during the opening rounds of the operation. (These turned up in April when the battalion also received its first supplies of the new PIAT (Projector, Infantry, Anti-Tank) anti-tank weapons to replace the Boys heavy rifle, a 0.55 inch calibre bolt-action magazine weapon with considerable weight and recoil force which had come into service in 1937 but was now obsolescent.) Minefields were also a problem, as was enemy artillery fire – in one attack eight men of D Company were killed as the battalion was preparing for the first combined attack with Eighth Army.

During the night of 22 March the final assault on Tunis began in the face of sustained German artillery fire. In the opening phases 6th Gordons held the division's right flank before being relieved a week later by 6th East Surrey Regiment; the Gordons' losses were 20 killed and 51 wounded. In the next phase of the fighting 6th Gordons came under the command of 24 Guards Brigade which needed to be reinforced for the attack on Djebel Bou Aoukaz on 29 April. A and D companies, under the command of Major A.G.I. Fleming, fought alongside 1st Irish Guards and succeeded in taking their objectives despite coming under sustained counter-attack – at one point a force of 20 German tanks attacked from the rear of the battalion's position in the Gab Gab Gap. During the action 30 casualties were sustained; amongst them was Major Fleming who was the senior of the battalion's pre-war officers. But by then the end was in sight. On 6 April Montgomery's forces had broken through at Wadi Akarit, having breached the Mareth Line a month earlier, and the coastal route to Tunis was open. Both the Gordons battalions had minor roles in the fighting at Wadi Akarit but they were both to the fore in the advance through the Mareth Line. Not that it was easy going for them or for any of the other Highland regiments. In his war memoirs Lieutenant Neil McCallum, 5/7th Gordons, left a vivid account of the sweltering conditions as the British Eighth Army continued its pursuit of the retreating Germans, adding that whereas they had the benefit of transport, the British soldiers travelled on foot:

> There was more marching, on feet soft with weeks of trench life. A hard rocky country. We marched past a large isolated house, glaringly white in the sun and from within its rough walls you could feel the invisible eyes watching. A robed Arab stood at a metal gate. The files of men marched past, boots grating on the rock, or lifting up white dust in chalky parts.

With the two armies converging on Tunis Axis resistance began to crumble – Rommel had already departed the battle front, leaving General Hans-Jürgen von Arnim in command – and amidst chaotic conditions the Germans capitulated on 12 May. The fighting in North Africa had finally come to an end.

NINE

The Second World War: 1943–45

The British victory at El Alamein was a turning point in the war. Not only were the church bells rung throughout Britain to celebrate the feats of the Eighth Army, but Montgomery had proved that the British soldier had nothing to fear in action against his German counterpart. Even so, it was only an interlude, if a welcome one. Giving a bloody nose to Rommel's Afrika Korps had provided a marvellous fillip for morale but it was not the end of the war. Ahead lay two and a half years of hard fighting and there was still much to do – in addition to dealing with the Japanese the Allies faced a determined and ruthless enemy in Europe, where the brunt of the fighting was being borne by the Red Army in the heartlands of the Soviet Union. For the British and US forces the next stage of the war involved the capture of Sicily as a precursor to the invasion of Italy, a move which would lead to the final securing of the Mediterranean, with its vital maritime routes to India and the Far East.

The Sicilian operation called for a British seaborne assault by Montgomery's Eighth Army between Syracuse and the Pachino peninsula on the island's south-eastern coast on 10 July, while the US I and II Armored Corps under Patton's command would land on a 40-mile front along the southern coast between Gela and Scoglitti and Licata on the left flank. There would also be an airborne assault carried out by the US 82nd Airborne Division and the British 1st Airborne Division to attack targets in the inland area and to secure the landing grounds. Once ashore, Montgomery planned to create a bridgehead and to secure the ports of Syracuse and Licata before moving rapidly north to take Messina, while Patton's forces covered the left flank.

SICILY

1st (new) and 5/7th battalions

Two battalions of Gordon Highlanders took part in the battle for Sicily and both went into the operation with the high morale that had been instilled by the successful outcome of the fighting in North Africa. However, the capture of the island was not the foregone conclusion that the Allies hoped it would be, and it was not until 16 August that the fighting came to an end. As part of XXX Corps 51st (Highland) Division landed on the south-east corner of the island with the 1st Canadian Division on the left and then pushed north towards Pachino. To 1st Gordons fell the task of maintaining the bridgehead and within a week the division had pushed 75 miles inland in what the 1st Gordons' War Diary described as 'a long and tiresome hike'. The first choke point was at the town of Sferro, which covered the road and railway to Catania and was guarded by the German Hermann Goering Division, which proved to be a formidable opponent. To Felix Barker, 5/7th Gordons, Sferro was 'nothing more than a handful of houses at a T-junction' but it proved to be an awkward position to attack:

> The name of the place was in such small type that you had to peer close to the map to read it. Sferro. Yes, according to the reports that was where the opposition was coming from. Sferro. Just a handful of houses. It was a little village of negligible importance, for years a lazy insignificant place housing a few poor peasants. Yet here destiny had decided that an important and bitter battle should be fought out. A little too fanciful perhaps to attribute it all to destiny! After all, as you could see from the map, it was really because the enemy had seen that the land rose quite steeply behind, providing excellent cover and concealment for its 17-millimetre guns.

The fighting began in extremely hot weather on 19 July, and it soon became apparent that the capture of Sferro would be no easy matter. Under heavy German shell-fire 5th Black Watch was pinned down and it took a great deal of effort to clear the town. During the fighting both 1st and 5/7th Gordons lost the use of their radio sets and were forced to use runners. Although the Germans withdrew a week later it was not the end of the fighting, as they took up strong defensive positions at Gerbini, six miles to the south-east, which contained an airfield as well as a railhead. The delays stymied Montgomery's plan to push rapidly up the eastern side of Sicily – Patton had made better progress on the left – and it was not until 2 August that the Allies were in a position to move jointly on Messina. By then the German and Italian high command had decided that the island was indefensible and had laid plans to begin the evacuation on 11 August. Sicily fell on 16 August but some of the gloss was taken off the victory when over 100,000 German and Italian soldiers plus 9,800 vehicles were evacuated across the Straits of Messina to fight again in Italy. In October, the two Gordon battalions returned to Britain with 51st (Highland) Division for the next operation, the invasion of France.

ITALY

6th battalion

At the beginning of December 1943 6th Gordons left Tunisia and landed at Taranto in southern Italy before heading north by train to Spinazzola, where the weather was foul – a rude surprise after the conditions in North Africa. At that stage of the war Italy had surrendered and the Allies had invaded the country through Reggio Calabria and Salerno to engage the defending German forces. Naples, too, had fallen but the Allies' attempts to move quickly on Rome had been blocked by the Germans along the Gustav Line, with the result that offensives were confined to the coastal flanks. In the centre the mountainous terrain and obstacles such as the rivers Garigliano and Liri made any advance difficult, and hopes for an early breakthrough quickly faded. To break the impasse it was decided to mount an amphibious operation which would land Allied forces at Anzio, behind the German defensive positions. Codenamed Operation Shingle, the idea was to use General John P. Lucas's US VI Corps to secure a beach-head and then to threaten the road to Rome which lay 30 miles to the north. Amongst the British formations taking part in the landings on 22 January was 1st Division which landed unopposed and advanced inland to consolidate its position. After weeks of rumours, 6th Gordons now knew their destination.

Unfortunately, Lucas then dithered, waiting for the build-up of his forces to be completed, and this allowed the Germans to react. When he eventually attempted to move inland at the end of January the way had been blocked and US VI Corps found itself stuck on the Anzio salient. On 3 February 6th Gordons came under exceptionally heavy artillery fire, which seemed to come from every direction and the battalion suffered accordingly: seven killed, 18 wounded and 329 missing. After the action it was found that C Company had ceased to exist and had to be rebuilt from scratch with untried replacements. By the end of the month the

German assault had failed to dislodge the Allies but they still came under sustained artillery bombardment from enemy positions in the nearby Alban Hills. This was a grim period for the Allies, as the push towards Rome had also faltered in the Liri Valley due to the German occupation of the monastery at Monte Cassino, the home of the Benedictine Order. It stood on high ground outside the town of the same name, and being partially occupied by German forces became the scene of fierce house-to-house and street-to-street fighting before being razed to the ground.

The stalemate was broken in mid-May when Cassino finally fell, opening the Liri Valley route, and at the same time US VI Corps managed to break out of the Anzio bridgehead. The road to Rome was now open and between 28 May and 4 June the advance did not falter. Following the fall of the Italian capital 6th Gordons went into reserve or as the regimental historian puts it, the men enjoyed 'an interval of real relaxation, with ample time for hot baths, the issue of clean clothing, and a general furbishing up'. There was also time for retraining in preparation for the next phase of the war in Italy, which took 6th Gordons north to Florence and the Apennines. The battalion arrived in the city on 16 August to take over the western sector from 3/15th Punjab Regiment and it soon found itself under fire from the remaining German positions to the north. It was a curious time, when action was interspersed with a semblance of normality, with the pipe band playing 'Retreat' in the city centre. Ahead lay the Allied advance into the mountainous areas to the north as the enemy grimly held on to its defensive positions along the Gothic Line, which stretched from Carrara in the west to Pesaro on the Adriatic. The attack began on 25 August with the US Fifth Army pushing towards Bologna while the British Eighth Army struck into the plains of Lombardy. The chain of command put 6th Gordons under US command as British XIII Corps was part of General Mark Clark's US Fifth Army. As the regimental historian notes, this was a new and difficult kind of fighting for those taking part in the operations:

> This was no country for tanks, and the lack of gun positions prevented effective artillery support, except on rare occasions. For the most part the infantry had to depend on their own weapons and their physical endurance; and a battalion could not fight as a battalion. Success depended on a series of company and platoon actions where subordinate commanders, down to section commanders, had to prove their worth.

It did not help that both the British and the US armies were being denuded to reinforce the operations in France and north-west Europe following the success of the invasion of Normandy earlier in the summer. The weather, too, worsened and as September gave way to October and November the battalion found itself fighting over some of the worst terrain experienced by British soldiers during the war in Europe. As the division advanced northwards its battalions were involved in further contact with the enemy at Presiola, Monte Gamberaldi, Monte Grande and Monte Castellaro. At the end of December the offensive was halted by the onset of severe winter weather, leaving 6th Gordons with three officers and 26 soldiers killed, five officers and 111 soldiers wounded and two officers and 26 soldiers missing. The campaign reopened in the spring but 6th Gordons was destined not to be a part of it. At the beginning of January 1st British Division was removed from the line and sent south to Taranto prior to being moved to Palestine, where the battalions began intensive training in river crossing and the use of armour. The end of the war in Europe and, later, in the Far East put paid to plans for any further deployments and it was not until later in the year that the battalion could begin demobilising its men.

NORMANDY AND NORTH-WEST EUROPE

1st, 2nd (new), 5/7th battalions

From the outset of US involvement in the Second World War their military planners had made a strong case for an early attack on the European mainland. In fact, the decision to press ahead with the invasion of north-west Europe had been taken as early as May 1943 at the Allied conference in Washington, and planning for it began under joint US–British direction immediately after the summit had ended. The main desiderata for the cross-Channel amphibious attack were quickly established: a landing area with shallow beaches and without obstacles which was within range of Allied air power, the neutralisation of local defences to allow a build-up which would equal the strength of the German defenders and the presence of a large port for reinforcement and re-supply. Deception also formed part of the plan: the idea was to persuade the Germans that the assault would be made across the narrowest part of the English Channel at Pas de Calais, where the beaches were shallow and led into the hinterland without the obstacles of cliffs and high ground. It also offered the opportunity to make a quick strike into the Low Countries and from there into Germany. All those reasons made Pas de Calais the ideal place for invasion, but because it was the obvious location it was quickly discounted, as the Allied planners realised that their German counterparts would deploy the bulk of their defensive forces there. By the end of the summer the plan was shown to the Allied leadership at the Quadrant conference in Quebec. The chosen landing ground was the Baie de la Seine in Normandy between Le Havre and the Cotentin peninsula, an area which met all the criteria, including a deepwater port at Cherbourg.

The initial planning called for an invasion force of three divisions, plus airborne forces which would create a bridgehead through which reinforcements could be landed quickly to break out into

Normandy and Brittany. Success would depend on the ability of the Allies to build up forces more rapidly than the Germans and with that in mind it would be essential to deny the enemy the chance to reinforce the landing grounds by destroying road and rail communications in northern France. Although Montgomery agreed with the main principles of the plan, he put forward an alternative proposal to attack in greater weight and along a broader front and with a larger airborne contribution. This was backed by Eisenhower, who activated his headquarters – Supreme Headquarters Allied Expeditionary Force (SHAEF) – in February. It was agreed that the initial assault should be made by five divisions, two US, two British and one Canadian, with one British and two US airborne divisions operating on the flanks. The D-Day invasion began on 6 June, with the airborne forces securing the flanks overnight while the main assault went in at dawn, preceded by a mighty bombardment from 2,000 warships in the Channel. By the end of the day the assault divisions were ashore and the five landing areas – Utah, Omaha, Gold, Sword and Juno – had been secured, with the loss of fewer than 10,000 casualties (killed, wounded or missing), less than expected.

None of the Gordon battalions was involved in the first wave of the assaults on D-Day but for all three the fighting in France and north-west Europe brought a variety of experiences. The battalions serving in the 51st (Highland) Division were part of the second wave of the invasion force which landed in France between 7 and 9 June, and to 5/7th Gordons fell the honour of being the first battalion to reach shore. Its first task was to secure the Oren bridgehead, which had been captured by airborne forces and which the Germans desperately wanted to retake. Almost immediately casualties began to be heavy as the Germans fought desperately to prevent the Allies from moving inland. The numbers killed in action were not particularly high but they occurred on a daily basis

– on 16 June the 5/7th's losses were seven killed and 24 wounded – and it soon became clear that it would be no easy matter to push inland.

In an attempt to break the deadlock British forces attacked west of Caen at the end of June (Operation Epsom), but were repulsed by the defending German II Panzer Corps. There was another setback on 11 July when 153 Brigade supported by 7th Black Watch attacked Colombelles village to the north-west of Caen. This was a particularly nasty battle, as the Germans had placed observation posts on the chimneys of the factory and were able to direct heavy and accurate fire onto the battalions as they went into the attack. The plan was for 1st Gordons to attack on the right with 5th Black Watch on the left, but despite encouraging initial reports the assault faltered and soon became unsustainable. The failure of the raid on Colombelles affected those taking part and when Major Martin Lindsay arrived as second-in-command a few days later the commanding officer, Lieutenant-Colonel Cumming Bruce, told him that the defences had been stronger than expected and that his men 'lacked offensive spirit as a result of being too tired, too much use having been made of the Division'.

After the failure of the Goodwood attack it became clear that 51st (Highland) Division had lost much of its fighting spirit due to exhaustion and the strain of being constantly in action, with the attendant high rate of casualties. So serious was the fall in morale that in mid-July Montgomery reported to the Chief of the Imperial General Staff that the 51st (Highland) Division was no longer 'battleworthy' and 'does not fight with determination'. As a result of this widespread slump in morale, which could have been disastrous for every regiment in the division, Montgomery was forced to sack its commander, Major-General Charles Bullen-Smith, late King's Own Scottish Borderers, who had succeeded Wimberley, on the grounds that 'the men won't fight for you'. It was a drastic move to make in the middle of a battle that had not yet been won, but although Montgomery was loath to make it he had no option. Bullen-Smith was replaced by Major-General T.G. Rennie, a former commanding officer of 5th Black Watch.

At the same time the division was taken out of the line for a short period of rest and recuperation at Cazelle, north-west of Caen, and some of the under-strength battalions were reinforced with fresh soldiers, many of them from English regiments. For example 5/7th Gordons received 46 reinforcements from The Duke of Wellington's Regiment, but they were quickly assimilated and soon became proud of the fact that they were 'Jocks' fighting with a distinguished Highland regiment. Ahead lay Operation Totalise, a thrust out of Caen towards Falaise mounted by the Canadian First Army with 51st (Highland) Division in support. Before the attack, which began on 8 August, Rennie reminded his senior officers that it could be 'the decisive battle in France' and that he expected every soldier in the division to show the same 'determination and offensive spirit' that they had demonstrated at Alamein. Although the Germans put up stout resistance Falaise fell on 16 August and the way to the River Seine was open. By then the 51st (Highland) Division had returned to its old form despite being frequent victims of 'friendly fire' from RAF strike aircraft even though yellow recognition panels were always displayed.

By then, 2nd Gordons had arrived in France as part of 15th (Scottish) Division which landed towards the end of June. The attacking forces immediately found themselves involved in heavy fighting against German positions on the Eterville Ridge south of Odon as part of Operation Epsom. (During the operations 2nd Gordons was brigaded with 10th Highland Light Infantry and 2nd Argyll and Sutherland Highlanders.) The operation began on 26 June in poor weather conditions with heavy rain which meant that there would only be limited air cover. When 2nd Gordons went into the attack a hail storm began and the drizzle continued throughout the day as 15th (Scottish) Division pushed towards the small town of Cheux. Armoured support was provided by 11th Armoured Division and 31 Tank Brigade but the presence of the tanks was often a mixed blessing, as they attracted heavy German defensive fire and added to the confusion, one watching staff officer noting that 'what little space was left in the lanes seemed to be filled by our own tanks, closed down and deaf to all appeals. None who was in Cheux that morning is likely to forget the confusion'. The fighting continued for a week before the division was withdrawn without achieving the expected breakthrough. Although Epsom was not a tactical success, it had taken the sting out of the German counter-attack and prevented German armour from driving a wedge between the Allied forces as they forced their way south into Normandy. During the fighting 2nd Gordons lost 254 casualties killed, wounded or missing. So heavy were the losses that the battalion was forced to make a temporary reduction from four to three rifle companies.

While these events were unfolding the stalemate was broken by Operation Cobra, mounted on 25 July by the US First Army, which pushed as far south as Avranches and the pivotal neighbouring town of Pontaubault. Suddenly the possibility opened of invading Brittany in the west and racing eastwards toward Le Mans and the River Seine. The task was given to seven divisions of Patton's US Third Army, which moved with exemplary speed into Brittany, frequently running ahead of their lines of communication as they sped into the open countryside. Bottlenecks and traffic jams were overcome by the simple expedient of despatching staff officers to forward positions with instructions to get the units through, regardless of their sequence in the battle plans. Within three days Patton's divisions were through the Avranches–Pontaubault gap; it was not a manoeuvre which would have been recognised at staff college, but it worked. At the same time, 2nd Gordons was involved in British moves from Caumont to Vire, where the battalion found itself fighting in 'real bocage country, undulating, close and intricate, with deep winding lanes, thick hedges, orchards, woods and copses, and patches of grazing land'. The regimental historian added that while it was hard going 'the Gordons appreciated their new environment, where milk and butter could be had in plenty and eggs were not hard to come by'. Best of all, the two attacks meant that the break-out from Normandy had finally begun and the Allies were free to sweep east and threaten the Seine valley and the approaches to Paris.

The next problem for the Allies was overstretch – as the attacking forces moved away from the beach-heads their supply lines became longer and that had an impact on the speed of their advance into north-west Europe. It also meant that the war would not end in 1944. In September the Highland Division took part in the operations to take the ports of Le Havre and Dunkirk but this was preceded by a highly emotional moment when St Valéry was retaken amid scenes of great local jubilation. Each brigade in the division was placed in roughly the same positions that had been occupied by their predecessors in 1940 and that evening (3 September) the massed pipes and drums played 'Retreat' outside the divisional headquarters at Cailleville. From there the advance took the division into Flanders and on into Holland where the flat 'polder' low lands had been flooded, causing inevitable problems. This included a period of intensive fighting as both the 15th (Scottish) Division and the 51st (Highland) Division fought their way over a succession of formidable water obstacles towards the River Maas. During the crossing of the Schelde–Maas Canal west of Donck on 15 September C Company of 2nd Gordons made the initial assault with the men wearing sandbags over their boots and carrying the minimum of equipment in order to maintain silence and create maximum surprise. Despite the precautions the men came under machine-gun fire and three Gordons were killed and 20 more were wounded.

It was at this stage of the battle, when the Allies were still confident that the end of the war was in sight and when conditions were at their worst, that the Germans decided to counter-attack in the Ardennes. The plan was the brainchild of Adolf Hitler who reasoned as early as September that the winter weather – 'night, fog and snow' – would give the Germans the opportunity to hit back at the Allies through the dense Ardennes forest, with its narrow steep-sided valleys, and then turn rapidly north to recapture Brussels and Antwerp. The attack would split the Allies, leaving the US armies unable to come to the aid of Montgomery's 21st Army Group, which would be encircled and destroyed before it could attack the Ruhr. It did not turn out that way but the Battle of the Bulge, as it came to be known, almost allowed the Germans to achieve their aims by creating a huge salient, or 'bulge', in the Allied lines. During the battle 51st (Highland) Division in XXX Corps supported the US Ninth Army in the Ourthe Valley. Although the winter conditions were severe, one Gordons officer offered the opinion that it was preferable to fight over 'snow-covered hills of great beauty' which provided 'a pleasant change from the mud of Holland'.

Ahead lay the equally ferocious fighting in the Reichswald, which housed part of the Siegfried Line, the heavily fortified German defensive position. The 51st (Highland) Division's objective on 8 February was the town and road and rail centre of Goch, which had to be taken to secure the southern sector of the Reichswald in preparation for the crossing of the Rhine. It was a hard-fought battle which involved close-quarter fighting and, according to those who were involved in both battles, it was preceded by the heaviest enemy bombardment since Alamein. In his memoirs Martin Lindsay provided a concise account of the tactics that were used, and his description explains how a brigade attack was planned and executed:

> 5th Black Watch were to start by taking all the main parts of the town [Goch] south of the river, up to and including the big square. The 5/7th Gordons were to pass through and take on beyond the square as far as the railway. 1st Gordons' objective was the area just south of the 5th Black Watch/5/7th Gordons boundary. This included the beginning of the main road to the south-west [Thomashof], with two road junctions, a school, a factory and several largish buildings in the area.

Matters went less smoothly for 1st Gordons when A Company was overrun due to lack of armoured support, and the battalion lost three officers and 21 soldiers killed and seven officers and 59 soldiers wounded. A further officer and 48 soldiers were posted as missing. The battle to take Goch lasted two days and it is rightly counted as a Gordons battlefield. One of several junior officers to win a Military Cross during the fighting in the Reichswald was 2nd Lieutenant Alexander Scott, 5/7th Gordons, who was a platoon commander in C Company. A wartime conscript from Aberdeen, he returned to academic life after the war and went on to become a leading poet and critic whose work in Scots was much praised. Later, he put his feelings about his time in the battalion into his poem 'Coronach For the Dead of the 5/7th Battalion The Gordon Highlanders':

> Waement the deid
> I never did,
> But nou I am safe awa

I hear their wae
Greetan greetan dark and daw,
Their death the-streen my darg the-day.

The eventual capture of Goch, followed by the fall of another strongpoint at Hekkens, opened the way for the Rhine crossing which was begun on 23 March 1945. According to Martin Lindsay, 'Montgomery was supposed to have said that Scottish troops were the best for assaulting' and the task was given to 15th (Scottish) and 51st (Highland) Divisions using Buffalo amphibious vehicles. During the operation 5/7th Gordons landed to the east of Rees on the opposite bank, but 1st Gordons followed 5th Black Watch in an operation which was delayed by the inability of the returning Buffaloes to climb out of the river. A description of the crossing was later written up by 1st Gordons for the regimental records:

> The buffaloes slowly crawled over the fields, then dipped into the water, became waterborne, and then one had the feeling of floating down out of control, yet each buffalo churned without difficulty out of Germany's greatest barrier and at the right place by the flickering green light. Once aground the buffaloes with vehicles took one 200 yards inland, those with troops deposited their load on the green fields, now baked hard by the recent fine weather, at the water's edge; two bunds [dykes] each about ten feet high stood against the skyline, otherwise the flatness was unbroken.

All the Scottish battalions got safely across the river but during the operation the 51st (Highland) Division suffered a tragedy when General Rennie was killed during a heavy German mortar attack near the town of Rees. It was a shattering blow, as Rennie had been a popular and inspiring commander. He was succeeded by Major-General Gordon MacMillan, an experienced and well-liked Argyll and Sutherland Highlander. (His son, John, commanded 1st Gordons in the 1970s. See Chapter Ten.)

To the south 2nd Gordons crossed the Rhine opposite the village of Wolffskath and took part in the advance towards Celle, with the ultimate objective being the crossing of the River Elbe and the capture of Lübeck. Once across the river the Scottish battalions found that the German defenders were in no mood to surrender and some units seemed to fight with a greater fanaticism as they fell back on the 'Fatherland'. Hitler Youth battalions proved to be particularly troublesome. When 2nd Gordons came across an uncompromising young woman who claimed that the Nazis would never surrender until every man was killed she received the dusty response 'that we were killing off Nazi soldiers with that purpose in view'. Nevertheless, the Rhine crossing was the beginning of the end and for the next month the 51st (Highland) Division was constantly on the move as it fought its way north towards Bremen and Bremerhaven, which was reached on 8 May. At the same time, 15th (Scottish) Division reached Gros Hansdorf to the north-east of Hamburg. For the Gordons and for the rest of the Allied armies the war in Europe was over, and ahead lay the task of restoring order to the shattered country. In Lübeck the 2nd battalion, under the command of Lieutenant-Colonel R.W.M. de Winton, found that the biggest problem was the huge number of displaced persons, who needed food and shelter, while the 1st battalion, commanded by Lieutenant-Colonel Grant Peterkin, moved to Neustadt near Hanover. For 5/7th Gordons (Lieutenant-Colonel C.F. Irvine) which had fought from El Alamein to the north German plain it was the end of the road. Ahead lay demobilisation and a return to Scotland before going into suspended animation and an uncertain future. The battalion's last flourish was a splendid parade in Munich, which was arranged by the US Army in the first week of June to return a drum which had been retrieved by the US 10th Armored Division during the drive into Germany. It was the only survivor of the 5th Gordons' drums, which had been stored at Metz before the retreat to St Valéry in May 1940.

BURMA

100th Anti-Tank Regiment (Gordon Highlanders), Royal Artillery, 116th Regiment (Gordon Highlanders) Royal Armoured Corps

Following Japan's decisive advances in south-east Asia and the fall of the key British bases at Hong Kong and Singapore, Japanese forces turned next to Burma, which was invaded from Raheng in Thailand early in 1942. Originally the Japanese had not been interested in occupying the whole country and believed that their strategic needs would be served by taking the port of Rangoon and the airfields on the Kra isthmus, but their minds were changed by two factors: the realisation that Britain could use Burma as a springboard in any attempt to retake Malaya, and also by the threatening presence of the Chinese 5th and 6th armies to the north along the lines of communication known as the Burma Road.

The Japanese plan called for a three-pronged attack – on Rangoon, the Salween River and the Sittan River – and as had happened in Malaya the attacking troops relied on speed and aggression. On 11 February they crossed the Salween, the retreating 17th Indian Division blew the bridges across the Sittang three days later and by 18 March Rangoon had fallen. Although the British and Indian forces counter-attacked in the Irrawaddy Valley at the end of the month, they were outflanked to the east and to the west where the Japanese drove General Chiang Kai-shek's army back towards the Chinese border. Short of supplies, exhausted and demoralised, the two armies went their separate ways and the

British and Indian forces began what came to be known as 'the longest retreat in British military history'. Following a march of 900 miles the survivors crossed over the border into India on 19 May: of the original 30,000, 4,000 were dead and another 9,000 were missing.

The reconquest of Burma is one of the great sagas in the histories of the British and Indian armies. It was the longest sustained campaign of the Second World War; it was fought over a harsh terrain which included deep jungle as well as desert and mountain; it was often war to the knife, with opposing soldiers caught in bitter close-quarter combat and those who surrendered were rarely granted much mercy. It began with a painful retreat and ended with a famous victory, which relied as much on the endurance and fortitude of the Allied troops as it did on the skill of their commanders. It involved soldiers from Britain, India, Burma, China, Nepal, the United States and West Africa, and because the campaign was almost as long as the war itself, it saw the introduction of innovations such as the use of air power in support of ground troops and modern radios to guide the strike and supply aircraft to their targets. While the Gordons did not provide infantry battalions for the Fourteenth Army – the famous 'Forgotten Army' commanded by Field Marshal Viscount Slim – two of its Territorial battalions fought in the Burmese theatre as anti-tank gunners and as an armoured regiment operating Sherman tanks.

Both battalions had had similar adventures since leaving the Clyde for destinations unknown. The 9th battalion arrived in Bombay towards the end of July 1942 and on their arrival at Sialkot the officers and men received the tidings that the battalion would be converted into an armoured regiment, serving in the Royal Armoured Corps as 116th Regiment (Gordon Highlanders). Although the pipe band continued in being and flashes of Gordon tartan were worn, 9th Gordons had become an armoured regiment and the men became 'troopers'. Slowly but surely the first tanks began to appear – elderly and under-gunned US Lee and Grant models – and it was not until the end of 1943 that the first modern Shermans arrived. The new regiment was assigned to 255 Tank Brigade in the 44th Indian Armoured Division. For the 8th battalion there was also a lengthy voyage to India by way of South Africa and as 100th (Gordon Highlanders) Anti-Tank Regiment, Royal Artillery 8th Gordons joined 2nd Division at Ahmednagar equipped with 6-pounder anti-tank guns. Later the new formation was re-equipped with 3-inch mortars so that it could also be used in the infantry role. There was further change at the end of 1943 when two Gordon batteries were transferred to 112th (Royal Warwickshire Regiment) Light Anti-Aircraft Regiment, Royal Artillery, in exchange for two batteries equipped with Bofors anti-aircraft guns. This entailed a further name-change to 100th (Gordon Highlanders) Light Anti-Aircraft and Anti-Tank Regiment, Royal Artillery.

In March 1944 the Japanese army made its long-expected attack on India when General Renya Mutaguchi opened a major offensive across the River Chindwin to attack Imphal and Kohima in Assam. This would give the Japanese the springboard to invade India, and for that reason it was imperative for the British and Indian forces not just to hold those two key points but also the railhead at Dimapur, which was the end of the supply line from India. Throughout the battle for Kohima, 2nd Division was heavily involved, with the guns and mortars of the Gordons supporting various positions. With batteries scattered over a large area it was impossible for the commanding officer, Lieutenant-Colonel D.B. Anderson, to maintain any central control so that individual commanders had to rely on their own judgement. One troop of mortars fired 600 rounds in a ten-hour period, fighting in a battle which broke the back of the attempted Japanese invasion.

By the beginning of 1945 the war in Burma was entering its

final phase and the Allies decided on a twin assault which saw Slim's Fourteenth Army attack the enemy on the line between Mandalay and Pakkoku (Operation Capital), while a second amphibious and airborne assault on Rangoon was planned at the beginning of 1945 (Operation Dracula). Slim's intention was to break out from the Kohima area and to make a four-pronged advance towards Indaw, Schwebo, Myinmu and Pakkoku. At the same time Lieutenant-General Sir Philip Christison's XV Corps would move into the Arakan to recapture the airfields, which would extend Allied air cover to Rangoon and the border with Thailand. The offensive opened on 3 December when the 11th East African Division and the 20th Indian Division crossed the Chindwin and began advancing with little sign of Japanese resistance. Faced by less opposition than he had expected, Slim decided to feint towards Mandalay while driving towards Meiktila, a key communications centre. Once the upper reaches of the River Irrawaddy had been seized, the way would be open to race south to Rangoon.

At this stage the Gordons armoured regiment entered the fray when it joined 7th Indian Division in its push towards Meiktila in December 1944. The regiment was in continuous action for a month and quickly discovered that operating a tank in extreme temperatures was a hazardous and exhausting business. At the beginning of April Meiktila, with its railhead and two airfields, fell into the hands of the advancing Fourteenth Army and at long last the road to Rangoon was open. During this phase the Gordons acted as a spearhead force for 5th Indian Division, together with 7th and 16th Cavalry and 3/9th Jat Regiment, all of the Indian Army. There was a close call at Pyinmana, where the bridge had been mined but the Japanese sapper charged with the task of blowing it up had fallen asleep and woke to find the British and Indian tanks making the crossing. By the time the war came to an end with the capitulation of Japan on 14 August the 116th Gordons were still in action, and to their men falls the honour of being the last armoured regiment to come out of action. By then 100th Gordons had returned to India to begin the process of demobilisation which accompanied the cessation of hostilities.

TEN

Cold War and Counter-Insurgency

The end of hostilities in Europe was greeted with widespread relief – Nazi Germany had proved to be an obstinate and unyielding enemy – but following the end of the war in Europe the fighting continued against the Japanese in Burma and the Pacific until mid-August. Fortunately, none of the Gordons battalions in Europe was earmarked for duty against the Japanese, but all three were involved in the complicated peace-enforcement and peace-making duties facing the Allies in post-war Germany. The bulk of these fell on the 1st battalion, which had ended the war in Bremerhaven and was destined to remain in post-war Germany until 1950. At the beginning of 1946 it moved to Muna Camp near Zeve, then on to Verden, before a more permanent posting to the industrial city of Essen on the Ruhr. Home to the huge Krupp industrial complex, the city had been the target for heavy aerial bombardment throughout the war and the damage to the infrastructure made life difficult for the Germans and the occupying forces alike. The 1st battalion was housed in the Meeanee Barracks, which one Gordon, writing with some feeling in the regimental magazine *Tiger and Sphinx*, described as 'a heap of steel, bricks and mortar'. After the excitement of the final weeks of victory it was a huge anticlimax and it proved to be a taxing time for the battalion, now under the command of Lieutenant-Colonel B.J.D. Gerrard. Eventually sporting activities were increased and the introduction of new and regular training routines kept men on their toes but the time at Meeanee Barracks was described by the regimental historian as 'monochromatic' and it tested to the full the battalion's *esprit de corps*.

A vivid description of the conditions faced by 1st Gordons during this period can be found in the private letters of the future novelist James Kennaway, who served with the battalion as a National Service subaltern. (These are contained in the Kennaway Archive in the National Library of Scotland.) The son of a Perthshire lawyer and factor, Kennaway had been commissioned as a Cameron Highlander in 1948 but due to the desperate shortage of junior officers had been posted to 1st Gordons. While his letters recorded the improving state of affairs in West Germany – rough shooting for the officers and cheap drink and cigarettes for every soldier – he could not ignore the local conditions and in one letter to his mother he described a little boy in Essen tripping over a boot in the snow: 'then, picking himself up, brushed his knees and ran on, assuredly that might happen in England and to any child. Only the boot still had a foot in it'. Kennaway later wrote about his time with 1st Gordons in his first novel, *Tunes of Glory*, whose plot centres on the clash of personalities between two officers – Jock Sinclair, an officer from the ranks with a superb wartime record who is replaced as commanding officer by Basil Barrow, a pre-war Regular officer. Before the novel was published Kennaway sent the manuscript to be read for accuracy by a brother officer, John Durbin, who replied that he could identify every single one of the officers in the fictional Campbell Barracks (loosely based on Queen's Barracks, Perth). Later the book was made into a memorable and highly acclaimed film of the same title, with Alec Guinness playing Sinclair and John Mills playing Barrow.

The reason for Kennaway's presence in the army was National Service. Under a succession of post-war National Service Acts every male citizen had to register at his local branch of the Ministry of Labour and National Service as soon as he became 18. Information about the relevant age-groups and clear-cut instructions were placed in the national newspapers and broadcast on BBC radio, and schools and employers passed on the relevant official information to their young charges. Short of deliberately refusing to register, there was no way the call-up could be ignored and those who did try to avoid conscription were always traced through their National Health records. Between the end of the war and the phasing-out of conscription in 1963 2.3 million men served as National Servicemen, the majority in the army. In its final form the period of conscription was two years (there had been earlier periods of 12 and 18 months) and, like every other regiment in the British Army, the Gordons benefited from the contribution made by men who were the first peacetime conscripts in British history.

By the time that Kennaway joined the Gordons in Essen the regiment had undergone one of the structural changes which have been visited on the British Army throughout its existence whenever war is replaced by peacetime conditions. At the end of the war against Nazi Germany, Italy and Japan, Britain was exhausted, physically and economically, and inevitably there was a need for immediate retrenchment. Fighting the war had cost the country £3,000 million and there remained a high level of debt arising from loans made by the USA during and after the conflict; exports had fallen to new levels and sterling was weak. Industry, too, was in turmoil as the incoming Labour government introduced a rapid policy of nationalisation of coal-mining, the railways and steel. Inevitably, the armed forces were not immune from the adverse economic conditions. Just over five million men and women were still in uniform and the army alone had 20 divisions, but it quickly became clear that the cost of maintaining those forces was beyond the reach of a country whose economy had been devastated by the war. As a result, cutbacks and scaling-down became the order of the day. By 1951 the size of the infantry had shrunk to 20 per cent of the army's total size – 88,100 soldiers out of a total strength of 417,800, all line-infantry regiments had been reduced to a single battalion, wartime Territorial battalions had been scrapped or amalgamated and the combat units had fallen to 184, consisting of 77 infantry battalions, eight Gurkha battalions, 69 artillery regiments and 30 armoured regiments.

In common with the other line-infantry regiments of the British Army, The Gordon Highlanders was forced to reduce its size to one battalion through the amalgamation of its 1st and 2nd battalions, with the latter being placed 'in suspended animation'. This allowed the old 2nd battalion to be run down and for those remaining to join the 1st battalion in Germany. At the same time the Territorial battalions were put into suspended animation until 1947, when the 5/7th battalion was amalgamated with the 6th battalion to form the 5/6th (Banff, Buchan and Donside) battalion, with company headquarters across the regiment's traditional recruiting area. At the same time the old 4th battalion, which had served as a machine-gun regiment during the war, was re-formed in the infantry role as 4/7th Gordon Highlanders (TA). Both the 8th and the 9th Territorial battalions were disbanded. Later, in 1961, the two remaining Territorial battalions were amalgamated to form 3rd Gordons. And later still it became part of the 2nd Battalion 51st Highland Volunteers.

Before all these changes took place a somewhat different experience had faced the 2nd battalion. As we have seen, it had ended the war on the road to Hamburg and Germany was to be its home for the first peacetime months, but change was in the air. In September 1945 the battalion returned to Britain, where the intention was to retrain it as airborne soldiers as part of 6th Airborne Division, already earmarked for service in Palestine. At the last minute there was a change of plan, and the battalion embarked for Tripoli. Despite the hot Mediterranean climate the posting turned out to be no picnic. An important strategic base for Allied interests during the Second World War, Tripoli was the seat of the British military administration which ruled the former Italian colonies of Tripolitania and Cyrenaica until they became independent in 1951 as the United Kingdom of Libya under the supervision of the United Nations (UN). Conditions were trying – the camp at Azzizia Barracks had not been completed – and the local amenities were not of the best. Sport took up a lot of the time and there were exercises with the fellow resident battalions, made memorable because field-firing used up tons of wartime ammunition, but as the regimental historian puts it, 'although the tenor of life in Tunisia was pleasant, there were few excitements'.

Fortunately, the experience was captured by another Gordons officer who later became a novelist – George Macdonald Fraser who had fought during the war in the 9th Border Regiment as a private soldier before being commissioned in 2nd Gordons. The creator of the Flashman novels – named after the bully in *Tom Brown's Schooldays* – Fraser also produced the equally memorable character of Private McAuslan, 'the biggest walking disaster to hit the British Army since Ancient Pistol'. Although Fraser claimed that 'the Highland battalion in this book [*The General Danced at Dawn*] never existed, inasmuch as the people in the stories are fictitious' it is equally clear that he based his tale on his time spent with 2nd Gordons. Reviewing the first collection in the *Sunday Times*, Bernard Fergusson, a distinguished Black Watch soldier and himself an author, said of McAuslan's creator: 'Twenty-five years have not dimmed Mr Fraser's recollections of those hectic days of soldiering after the war.' Later, in 1988, after publishing the third collection, *The Sheikh and the Dustbin*, Fraser finally acknowledged the debt he owed to his old regiment in the creation of his short stories when he dedicated the volume to his commanding officer, Lieutenant-Colonel R.G. Lees, following a chance meeting at a book-signing in London.

In May 1947 2nd Gordons left Port Said on board the troopship *Devonshire* and returned home, to be stationed in Edinburgh at Duddingston Camp, Portobello, where the men carried out a range of different activities, from helping to bring in the potato crop, through training cadets, to mounting a Royal Guard while the king was resident at Balmoral. Following a peripatetic existence with battalion headquarters at Comrie in Perthshire and the rifle companies scattered across Lowland Scotland, 2nd Gordons found its last home at Easthaven near Arbroath, in a barracks which had been used by the Women's Royal Naval Service. From there the remnants proceeded to Germany where the amalgamation parade took place at Essen on 12 July 1948. Predictably perhaps, the day dawned with torrential rain and the actual ceremony was carried out in the barracks' gymnasium.

1ST BATTALION THE GORDON HIGHLANDERS

While the amalgamation of the two Gordon battalions did not cause the turmoil that accompanied the joining together of two different regiments, the moment was tinged with sadness for the disappearance of names which harked back to the 75th and the 92nd, the founding fathers of the modern regiment. It helped matters that the first commanding officer, Lieutenant-Colonel V.D.G. Campbell, was not a Gordon but a Cameron Highlander and, untouched by earlier loyalties, he made it his business 'to make everyone realise that we were now the 1st Battalion The Gordon Highlanders, incorporating and carrying on all the best traditions of the former Regiments in the one battalion'. It also helped that shortly after the amalgamation the new battalion moved to Berlin in May 1949 to take the place of 1st Worcestershire Regiment. Not only did this posting provide a pleasant change of scene after the rigours of Essen and Tripoli, but it took the battalion right into the heart of a growing confrontation with the Soviet Union, which came to be characterised as the Cold War.

At the end of the Second World War the Allies had taken the decision to partition Germany. Although the former capital, Berlin, was in the eastern Communist sector it too was divided and the relationships between the wartime Allies became strained and fractious. The year before 1st Gordons arrived in the former German capital a quarrel over currency reform had encouraged the Soviets to introduce a blockade, a move that was clearly meant to overawe the Allies. At the time the Soviets had 18,000 soldiers in their sector while the Allies had only 6,500, and to reinforce that superiority the Soviets could also rely on another 300,000 troops in the east German zone of occupation. The crisis had been resolved by an audacious airlift of goods – at one point an Allied aircraft landed in Berlin every three minutes – but due to continuing Soviet intransigence the airlift continued for 11 months and 1st Gordons found itself caught up in the trying local conditions. Despite those difficulties the battalion was still able to take part in an important ceremonial event when it sent a large detachment plus drums and pipes to take part in a parade on 20 August 1949 to mark the granting of the Freedom of the City of Aberdeen, a signal honour. Also taking part in the parade were 4/7th and 5/6th battalions and representatives from The London Scottish.

The Berlin deployment ended in April 1950 when 1st Gordons moved to Sennelager in Westphalia, but this proved only to be a brief interlude. After almost six years of peacetime soldiering in Europe the battalion exchanged the north German plain for the heat of the jungles of Malaya. It proved to be an abrupt change because not only was the battalion moving into different climatic conditions but it was also going into what was already a difficult and dangerous operational zone. During the Second World War the country had been overrun and captured by the Japanese army, which then garrisoned it with 100,000 troops. The only opposition came from mainly Malay-Chinese guerrilla groups which mounted a limited number of attacks against Japanese installations with the support of Force 136, a British-backed counter-insurgency group. At the end of the war this Malayan People's Anti-Japanese Army was transformed into the Malayan Races Liberation Army (MRLA), the military wing of the Chinese-controlled Malayan Communist Party (MCP). Initially Britain planned a Malayan Union which would have given the Chinese citizenship rights but this was opposed by the Malay political élite and the result was the creation of a Malayan Federation in which Chinese rights were sacrificed to the interests of the Malay rulers. As a result of the heightened political tensions, the Chinese Communists' opposition turned into an armed struggle in 1948, the MCP was declared illegal and some 10,000 MRLA fighters moved into the jungle to mount guerrilla operations against the civilian population and the security forces under their military commander Chin Peng.

Initially the idea was to drive the terrorists (known as CTs, for 'Communist Terrorists') into the jungle away from urban populations, but this changed in April 1950 with the appointment of Lieutenant-General Sir Harold Briggs as Director of Operations 'to plan, co-ordinate and direct the anti-bandit operations of the police and fighting services'. To achieve those ends Briggs integrated the efforts of the police and the military and reorganised the intelligence services to provide him with information about terrorist movements and to infiltrate the Communist cadre infrastructure. A 'food denial' policy was also instituted, but the main obstacle was the support given to the MRLA by the Chinese inhabitants of the jungle. The solution was the resettlement of 650,000 villagers in 550 New Villages – secure areas where they would enjoy a safe and profitable environment away from MRLA influence. Then it was the task of the infantry to move into the jungle, to secure bases and drive the CTs into the deeper and less hospitable depths, and this is what awaited 1st Gordons when it arrived in Singapore on 4 April 1951. It was the first time the regiment had been in the colony for ten years and the men were immediately given intensive training in the niceties of jungle warfare.

By the middle of May the training was deemed to have worked and the battalion was moved to its new stations in Malaya – Headquarters at Kuantan, A and D Companies at Jabor and Gambang and B and C Companies at Jerantut and Kuala Krau. While patrolling in the jungle, the first thing that struck the men of 1st Gordons was its frighteningly large scale. The trees, forming an unbroken canopy, often reached two hundred feet, their leaves could be as large as warriors' shields; and all around the base crazy patterns of creepers and roots constructed obstacles that were well-nigh impassable but for brute force and razor-sharp parangs, or machetes. Underfoot rotting leaves and undergrowth produced a soft mushy surface frequently traversed by meandering streams which turned what footholds there were into a spongy swamp. As the men of 1st Gordons discovered, these operations demanded strength, stamina and determination as well as a steady nerve. Writing in the regimental magazine, *Tiger and Sphinx*, 2nd Lieutenant John Comyn provided a glimpse of what could happen on a regular patrol into the jungle:

> It was pitch black (no moon) and you couldn't see your own hands – still less the man in front of you, so you had to hold onto his equipment. By the time we had found the rest of the Platoon the guide had really lost his bearings and we were bashing along a track making a hell of a noise – I was horrified but there it was. Suddenly a torch shone on us from another track about five yards away only. We stopped dead and pushed safety catches forward expecting an ambush.

In the darkness of the jungle it was all too possible that Comyn and his men had made contact with CTs but anticlimax followed – the torchlight came from locally recruited 'Kampong Guards' which had been formed to offer a measure of protection to Malay villages. It did not always turn out that way: the actual fighting against the CTs usually involved short-lived and unexpected firefights against a determined enemy. Perhaps the most unusual engagement took place at the end of 1951, when what was described as 'a motley collection' of Gordons found themselves caught up in the action. As the *Tiger and Sphinx* commented at the time, it was a bizarre occurrence:

> No man should normally be required, even in this war of nerves, to find himself, some two hours into deep jungle, surrounded by a hostile party consisting of an orderly room sergeant, a bandsman, a telephone switchboard operator, an armourer's mate, an intelligence sergeant, a release clerk, an MT corporal, HQ Company's store man and the Intelligence Officer, complete with map and pins.

The next year opened with a series of setbacks, the worst being the deaths of seven Gordons in an ambush, the heaviest single loss in the battalion's tour. This was balanced by a satisfactory number of 'kills' – to help underline the idea that on one level the war was an impersonal activity most of the resident infantry battalions kept a score-sheet of terrorists killed. During the final part of the deployment 1st Gordons was based at Tampin and enjoyed a period retraining in Singapore, where the battalion was based in the Selarang Barracks, ironically the home of the 2nd battalion at the beginning of the Second World War. In March 1954 the battalion left Negri Sembilan for Singapore, where it joined the troopship *Empire Fowey* for the voyage home. It had been a lengthy and gruelling campaign which had required discipline and firmness while fighting in a difficult and challenging environment. It also came at a price: during the three-year tour of duty 1st Gordons' casualties (killed in action) were four officers, one attached officer, two non-commissioned officers and 12 soldiers. It was not until 31 July 1960 that the 'emergency' in Malaya was declared to have ended.

On the return to Britain the regiment exercised its right to march through Aberdeen with 'bayonets fixed, drums beating and colours flying', a result of the earlier granting of the Freedom of the City. Fittingly, the parade took place on the anniversary of the Battle of Waterloo and equally fittingly, as the *Press and Journal* reported, the people of the city responded with a massive display of enthusiasm for the local regiment.

> It was for the jungle fighters of the 1st battalion, back from three years in Malaya, that the tremendous crowds reserved their greatest ovation . . . Three-quarters of an hour before the start of the march, the pavements of Union Street were well crowded with spectators. When the march began they were packed solid, every vantage point overlooking the route claimed by eager onlookers. Then came one of the most thrilling moments of the day as the massed Pipes and

> Drums of the Regiment came into view – the first time in the history of the Regiment that the five Battalion bands had marched and played together. Six abreast, regimental pride in every step, they swung down Union Street to the stirring strains of the Cock o' the North. And behind them, fluttering proudly, were the Queen's Colour and the Regimental Colour, with its battle honours going back over 160 historic years.

The battalion's period of home service lasted until the late summer of 1955 when, at extremely short notice, 1st Gordons was airlifted by RAF Transport Command to Cyprus. As the regimental historian noted: 'It was to be no holiday.' The island had been in British possession since 1878, when it was envisaged as a second Malta, a strategic base in the Mediterranean which would help to protect the Suez Canal and provide a stepping-stone to the Middle East. After the First World War, in 1925, Cyprus became a British Crown Colony governed by a legislative council. Within four years though there was trouble involving the local population and three main groups had emerged, all with differing political ambitions. The Turkish minority favoured British rule until such time as the new Turkish republic could look after their interests. The Orthodox Church represented the leadership of the majority Cypriot Greeks and favoured autonomy, while a minority group demanded union or '*enosis*' with Greece and by the 1930s was prepared to use violence to achieve its aims. In the post-Second World War period Cyprus quickly became a new battleground as Greek Cypriot guerrillas formed themselves into an underground army, *Ethniki Organosis Kypriakou Agonos* (EOKA, or the National Organisation of Greek Fighters) under the command of Colonel Georgios Grivas, and the unrest spilled over into violence and civil disobedience.

The 1st battalion arrived in Cyprus in October 1955 and quickly moved onto an operational footing, with battalion headquarters and A and B companies based at Xeros on the north-west coast while C and D companies operated in the Troodos Mountains. They quickly settled into a routine which consisted of searches for hidden weapons and operations in support of the police force. The Gordons' arrival coincided with the appointment of Field Marshal Sir John Harding as governor, and he began employing the same counter-insurgency methods which had proved so successful in Malaya. Operations against EOKA were intensified with offensive sweeps and drives and a state of emergency was declared in November. Throughout the campaign the main danger came from EOKA terrorists using grenades and bombs and in some respects, the military situation in Cyprus was to be an uneasy forerunner of later operations in Northern Ireland. Tragically for the battalion, the highest number of casualties occurred during a forest fire which swept through the Troodos Mountains in June 1956, killing 13 Gordons. The period of service ended in December, when the battalion left Cyprus and returned to Britain on board the troopship *Empire Orwell*. Ahead lay a brief stay at Old Park Barracks in Dover before moving back to Germany for three years at Celle near Hanover. By then National Service was coming to an end, making the regiment totally reliant on volunteers, but this was balanced by improvements in pay and conditions and by the introduction of more serviceable and smarter uniforms, including Number 2 service dress to replace the old Number 5 battle dress.

Following the deployment with the British Army of the Rhine (BAOR) the battalion moved to something completely different: a series of counter-insurgency operations which took them to east Africa (Kenya, Zanzibar and Swaziland) between 1962 and 1964, the East Indies (Borneo and Sarawak) between 1965 and 1966, and the first of many tours of duty in Northern Ireland following an eruption of violence in the province in 1969. The latter campaign, known as Operation Banner, was to be the longest lasting and did not officially come to an end until 31 July 2007, but the earlier deployments were also strenuous and dangerous operations. When the battalion moved to Kenya it was participating in the wider British policy of establishing a regional base after Kenya obtained independence a year later (1963), but the Gordons soon discovered that they were not about to enjoy a quiet life. In June 1962 there was an outbreak of violence in Swaziland and 1st Gordons was flown in to deal with it and restore order. The mood was tense and anxious: a few years earlier Kenya had suffered the depredations of the Mau Mau rebellion and there were fears that the flare-up in Swaziland could lead to similar lawlessness. Shortly before the battalion's tour of duty came to an end it provided a detachment to take part in Zanzibar's independence celebrations on 9 December, but the glitter was taken off the occasion when a month later the Sultan was deposed in a bloody coup.

Following a short tour in Scotland which was used to organise a number of recruiting drives the battalion moved back to the Far East in the summer of 1965. Trouble had broken out three years earlier over the future of Britain's three remaining colonies in the area – Sarawak, Brunei and Sabah – all of which constituted British Borneo. The prime minister of Malaya, Tunku Abdul Rahman, wanted to include them in a new Malayasian Federation but this was opposed by President Ahmed Sukarno of Indonesia, who wanted to incorporate the colonies into a greater Indonesia. The first trouble broke out in Brunei at the end of 1962 but although the rebellion against the sultan was crushed with British support, Sukarno opened a new offensive which became known as the 'Borneo confrontation'. There was a rapid escalation in the violence along the 970-mile land frontier and by the time 1st Gordons arrived the British contingent in the region had grown to

13 infantry battalions, one battalion of Special Air Service regiment, two regiments each of artillery and engineers, 40 strike aircraft and 80 helicopters as well as local police and border security force units. Throughout the operation the tactics were similar to those which had been used in Malaya in the previous decade but in this case greater use was made of helicopters to dominate the jungle.

When the battalion arrived it relieved 45 Commando Royal Marines at Kalabaken on the swamp eastern seaboard of Sabah. As happened in other post-war deployments the companies were split up and, according to the commanding officer Lieutenant-Colonel R.W. Smith, the men quickly came to grips with a situation which would have been familiar to anyone who served in Malaya:

> It was a junior leaders' war and the worth of those junior leaders was soon tested and assessed. The area was relatively quiet and was a good nursery slope on which to give the battalion its baptism of fire. The enemy – the Indonesians – were, like us, thin across the ground and reckoned not to be adventurous but, on the other hand, were of proved quality – mostly marines. The ground was marshy and the coastline deeply indented with lagoons, inlets and rivers. Inland, particularly towards the west of our front, was completely uncharted and bordered on what was known as 'The Gap', primeval jungle which had never been trod by man.

Patrolling these inhospitable areas dominated the battalion's tour of duty, which came to an end in the following year after Sukarno was removed from power in a military coup, allowing the confrontation to come to an end on 11 August 1966. As a result 1st Gordons returned to Scotland to take over from 1st Cameronians the responsibility for carrying out public duties. In April 1967 the battalion moved to Minden, where it formed part of 11 Brigade in the 1st Division. Within two years of the deployment a worrying new development saw violence breaking out in Northern Ireland and it would soon involve every regiment in the British Army, including The Gordon Highlanders.

The trouble in the province had begun in July as a result of the breaking-up of a civil rights march in Londonderry in which the Protestant paramilitary police (B-Specials) used considerable violence against the largely Catholic protesters. As the violence spread and Catholics across the province found themselves under attack by groups of Protestants, the decision was taken to reinforce the Northern Ireland garrison with additional soldiers acting 'in aid of the Civil power'. Initially they were made welcome, especially by the Catholic community, but the good relations did not last, particularly after the rump of the Irish Republican Army (IRA) entered the fray. In 1972 1st Gordons embarked on its first emergency tour of duty, and it was to be a baptism of fire. During the tour the battalion lost three soldiers killed by a booby trap while searching a house in Armagh on 18 June. An editorial note in the *Tiger and Sphinx* in 1973 gives some idea of the challenges facing commanding officers, in this case Lieutenant-Colonel (later Lieutenant-General Sir) John MacMillan:

> The Commanding Officer's policy was to dominate the area [Belfast's Andersonstown] by foot patrols, which in turn by using their eyes and ears and chatting up locals, would also produce the background knowledge on the area and its people – so vital from the intelligence aspect. At all times soldiers were to be polite and fair so that we did not make unnecessary enemies and indeed made friends where this was possible. From this it was hoped intelligence sources could be developed which would

> give us information and help remove the terrorist, thereby dominating the area using precise methods and not blind swipe operations. Intelligence as always was the key, and tied in very carefully with this was a considerable Civil Affairs campaign designed to give people confidence in the local civil authorities and a Public Relations campaign aimed at hitting back at, and countering IRA propaganda.

For the British Army Northern Ireland was soon to become familiar territory as its regiments began the long cycle of six-month roulement tours or longer accompanied deployments of up to two years. Each one brought its own challenges in helping to keep the peace while maintaining a sense of proportion in one of the most difficult and long-lasting counter-insurgency wars fought by the British Army.

For the next two decades the life of the 1st battalion was dominated by deployments in Germany interspersed with tours of Northern Ireland. This meant that there had to be a good deal of juggling between the demands made by mechanised warfare in the event of a major war breaking out in northern Germany against the Soviet Union and its Allies, and the need to train for low-intensity warfare in the streets and country places of Northern Ireland. While this added to the variety of a soldier's experience, it was a challenge for the regiment and often placed strains on family life. But it was not all West Germany and Northern Ireland. In 1974 1st Gordons served a tour of duty in 28 Infantry Brigade in Singapore, the fourth time that the regiment had been stationed in the Far East. Six years later the battalion made a welcome return to a home posting in Scotland and during this time the men had the unusual experience of serving as emergency prison warders at Frankland Prison in Durham, a new maximum-security facility. During this period 1st Gordons undertook a six-month tour of

Belize (formerly British Honduras) and then it was back to West Germany in the spring of 1983 to become a mechanised infantry battalion based at Deilinghofen. This was followed by a spell in the airmobile role.

Although the battalion was not deployed in Operation Granby, the British contribution to the US-led coalition which ousted Iraqi forces from Kuwait in 1991 following Saddam Hussein's illegal invasion the previous year, Gordon Highlanders did take part in the British war effort. The regimental band served with 32 Field Hospital and 28 men served in 7th Armoured Brigade's headquarters. After the Gulf War 1st Gordons moved to Berlin, but from the regimental records it is possible to see the extent of the battalion's workload during this period. Platoons were sent to reinforce other battalions in Northern Ireland and the Balkans and in 1993 the *Tiger and Sphinx* noted that: 'Groups of Gordons have ventured far and wide, to places such as Bosnia, Denmark, Sardinia, Canada, Cambodia, Norway, Austria and all over Germany . . . Needless to say, the Gordons' cap badge has been seen and worn with pride throughout the world.'

It would not be for much longer that the stag's head badge and the motto 'bydand' would enjoy that pre-eminence. In response to the end of the Cold War following the disintegration of the Soviet Union and the reunification of the two Germanys the Conservative government produced a Defence White Paper, *Options for Change*, which proposed that the army should be reduced from 155,000 to 116,000 soldiers and that the infantry should lose 17 of its 55 battalions. In Scotland the regiments selected for amalgamation were The Royal Scots with The King's Own Scottish Borderers and Queen's Own Highlanders with The Gordon Highlanders. It was accepted that Scottish regiments would be affected but because most of the Scottish regiments had served in the Gulf the decision came as a shattering blow and immediate steps were taken to fight it. A well-organised and high-profile 'Keep Our Scottish Battalions' campaign was initiated under the chairmanship of Lieutenant-General Sir John MacMillan, a Gordon Highlander and a former GOC Scotland, and the amalgamation of the two Lowland regiments was cancelled on 3 February 1993, together with the proposed amalgamation of the Cheshire and Staffordshire Regiments.

However, the second Scottish amalgamation was ordered to proceed, even though it was only 34 years since the earlier amalgamation of The Seaforth and Cameron Highlanders. Following lengthy discussions between the two regiments it was agreed that the new regiment would be known as The Highlanders (Seaforth, Gordons and Camerons) and that its form of dress, traditions and battle honours would reflect the histories of the constituent regiments. As a result the new regiment retained the Queen's Own Highlanders' cap badge with the Seaforth motto *Cuidich 'n Righ* and to reflect the importance of the tartans, all three were perpetuated in the new formation. All soldiers, less pipers and drummers, would wear the Gordon tartan kilt and a patch of Cameron tartan in the Tam o' Shanter bonnet; the pipers and drummers would wear the Cameron kilt with a patch of Gordon tartan in the bonnet; and the whole regiment would wear trews of Mackenzie tartan. At the end of 1993 1st Gordons left Berlin and moved into Dreghorn Barracks in Edinburgh in preparation for the amalgamation, which was fixed for 17 September 1994. During the summer a number of farewell events took place including a Trooping the Colour ceremony held at Smeaton Park in Aberdeen on 25 June 1994 which was attended by the colonel-in-chief, Prince Charles, Prince of Wales and Duke of Rothesay. Three days before the amalgamation parade the two regular battalions took part in a ceremony on the bridge at Craigellachie on the River Spey, a picturesque and historic location which marks one of the boundaries of the two regimental areas.

1ST BATTALION THE HIGHLANDERS (SEAFORTH, GORDONS AND CAMERONS)

Following the amalgamation 1st Battalion The Highlanders moved to Northern Ireland for a tour of duty, latterly in Londonderry, which ended in April 1997. Its next posting was to Somme Barracks in Catterick, Yorkshire, where it formed part of 19 Mechanised Brigade. Between then and its return to Edinburgh in March 2001 the battalion supplied reinforcements for other infantry regiments serving in the Balkans (Bosnia and Kosovo) and carried out a six-month tour of duty in Armagh between June and December 2000. During this period the battalion was involved in two operations providing aid to the civil community – helping to coordinate measures to combat an outbreak of foot-and-mouth disease in 2002 and acting as emergency firefighters during the strike of 2003. In March 2004 the battalion moved to Fallingbostel in Germany to join 7 Armoured Brigade, and began training with the Warrior armoured fighting vehicle. Between November 2005 and May 2006 1st Highlanders served in Basra in southern Iraq as part of Britain's military commitment to the forces in the country following the US-led operations to depose Saddam Hussein in 2003. Before the deployment, the regiment's future was already in doubt as a result of far-reaching reforms of the future structure of the infantry instigated by the Strategic Defence Review of July 2004. This time the change was even more radical as it involved the reduction of the size of the infantry from 40 to 36 battalions, and that signalled the end for the remaining 19 single-battalion regiments. In their place large regiments consisting of several battalions were formed (a move that had begun in the 1960s); in Scotland this new formation was called The Royal Regiment of Scotland and The Highlanders formed its 4th battalion, serving as The Highlanders, 4th Battalion The Royal Regiment of Scotland. Formation day for the new regiment was 28 March 2006 while the battalion was still in Basra where one of its antecedents, 1st Seaforth, had served 90 years earlier. Although the moment was tinged with great sadness, that sense of history helped to create part of the 'golden thread' which binds the future of the new regiment to the past histories and glories of its constituent parts.

Appendix

REGIMENTAL FAMILY TREE

1st battalion (75th)

1787: 75th (Highland) Regiment (Abercromby's)
1809: 75th Foot
1862: 75th Stirlingshire Regiment
1881: 1st battalion, The Gordon Highlanders
1948: amalgamation with 2nd battalion

2nd battalion (92nd)

1794: 100th (Highland) Regiment
1798: 92nd (Highland) Regiment
1803: 2nd battalion raised
1814: 2nd battalion disbanded
1861: 92nd (Gordon Highlanders)
1881: 2nd battalion, The Gordon Highlanders
1948: amalgamation with 1st battalion

75th/92nd

1948: 1st battalion, The Gordon Highlanders

1994: 1st The Highlanders (Seaforth, Gordons and Camerons) following amalgamation of Queen's Own Highlanders with The Gordon Highlanders

2006: The Highlanders, 4th Battalion, The Royal Regiment of Scotland

REGIMENTAL BADGE

The badge of The Gordon Highlanders was introduced in 1872 to replace an earlier badge, the Sphinx with the legend 'Egypt' which commemorated the service of the 92nd Highlanders in that country in 1800–01. The new badge commemorated the regiment's links with the Gordon family, being the crest of the Marquis of Huntly, later Duke of Gordon: a stag's head above a ducal coronet within a wreath of ivy and below the motto 'Bydand', a Scots word meaning 'biding, or abiding in the sense of enduring, lasting or biding the time'.

REGIMENTAL TARTANS

The regiment's tartan is the distinctive Gordon Highlander tartan which is the government or Black Watch tartan with a yellow stripe. It was designed originally for the Gordon Fencibles by William Forsyth, a tartan manufacturer in Huntly who remarked that the result looked 'very lively'. The 75th wore the government tartan until 1809, when it lost its Highland status.

REGIMENTAL PIPE MUSIC

Pipers were not officially recognised by the army until 1854 when all Highland regiments were allowed a Pipe-Major and five pipers. Before that most Highland regiments employed pipers as a regimental expense and these were distributed throughout the regiment disguised on the muster roll as 'drummers'. The pipes and drums were always fully trained infantry soldiers and were in addition to the military band which existed until 1994.

The regiment's pipe music is regularised as follows:
March past in quick time: The Cock o' the North
March past in slow time: St Andrew's Cross
The Charge: The Haughs o' Cromdale
Headquarters Company: My Nut-Brown Maiden
A Company: The Atholl Highlanders
B Company: The Inverness Gathering
C Company: The Back of Benachie
D Company: The Black Bear
Support Company: Bonnie Dundee

BATTLE HONOURS

Two Colours are carried by the regiment, the King's or Queen's, which is the Union flag. In the centre, on a crimson background, is the regimental badge surrounded by the name of the regiment, and encircled by a wreath of thistles, roses and shamrocks, with the regimental motto 'Bydand'. Emblazoned on the Regimental Colour, which is buff with a gold fringe, is a Royal Tiger superscribed with the word INDIA and a Sphinx superscribed with the word EGYPT.

During the Napoleonic wars battle honours were added to the colours. In their final form, those gained during the First World War and the Second World War are carried on the Queen's Colour and the remainder are carried on the Regimental Colour. At the outset battle honours were given sparingly or even randomly: in 1882 the system of battle honours was revised by a War Office committee under the chairmanship of General Sir Archibald Alison. It laid down guidelines whereby only victories would be included and the majority of the regiment had to be present. Additional refinements were made in 1907 and 1909 and their recommendations form the basis of the regiment's pre-1914 battle honours.

Pre-1914 (75th and 92nd)

Mysore	**Orthes**	**Tel-el-Kebir**
Seringapatam	**Peninsula**	**Egypt 1882, 1884**
Egmont-op-Zee	**Waterloo**	**Nile 1884–85**
Mandora	**South Africa 1835**	**Chitral**
Corunna	**Delhi 1857**	**Tirah**
Fuentes d'Onor	**Lucknow**	**Defence of Ladysmith**
Almarez	**Charasiah**	**Paardeberg**
Vittoria	**Kabul 1879**	**South Africa 1899–1902**
Pyrenees	**Kandahar 1880**	
Nive	**Afghanistan 1878–80**	

The First World War (21 battalions)

After the First World War there were further refinements to take cognisance of the size and complexity of the conflict. It was agreed that each regiment could carry ten major honours on their King's Colour but supporting operations would also receive battle honours which would not be displayed. The battle honours in bold type are carried on the Queen's Colour.

Mons	Albert 1916, 1918	St Quentin
Le Cateau	Bazentin	Bapaume 1918
Retreat from Mons	Delville Wood	Rosières
Marne 1914, 1918	Pozières	Lys
Aisne 1914	Guillemont	Estaires
La Bassée 1914	Flers-Courcelette	Hazebrouck
Messines 1914	Le Transloy	Bethune

Armentières 1914
Ypres 1914, 1915, 1917
Langemarck 1914
Gheluvelt
Nonne Boschen
Neuve Chapelle
Frezenberg
Bellewaarde
Aubers
Festubert 1915
Hooge 1915
Loos
Somme 1916, 1918

Ancre 1916
Arras 1917, 1918
Vimy 1917
Scarpe 1917, 1918
Arleux
Bullecourt
Pilckem
Menin Road
Polygon Wood
Broodseinde
Poelcapelle
Passchendaele
Cambrai 1917, 1918

Soissonais-Ourcq
Tardenois
Hindenburg Line
Canal du Nord
Selle
Sambre
France and Flanders 1914–18
Piave
Vittorio Veneto
Italy 1917–18

The Second World War (8 battalions)

In 1956 it was agreed to treat the Second World War in the same way. Those in bold type appear on the Queen's Colour.

Withdrawal to Escaut
Ypres-Comines Canal
Dunkirk 1940
Somme 1940
St Valéry-en-Caux
Odon
La Vie Crossing
Lower Maas
Venlo Pocket

Rhineland
Reichswald
Cleve
Goch
Rhine
North-West Europe 1940, 1944–45
El Alamein
Advance on Tripoli

Mareth
Medjez Plain
North Africa 1942–43
Landing in Sicily
Sferro
Sicily 1943
Anzio
Rome
Italy 1944–45

Allied and affiliated regiments

Canada

48th Highlanders of Canada

The Toronto Scottish Regiment

Australia

5/6th Battalion Royal Australian Infantry

1st Battalion Royal Victoria Regiment

South Africa

The Cape Town Highlanders

WINNERS OF THE VICTORIA CROSS

Private Thomas Beach, 92nd Highlanders, Crimean War, 1854

The regiment's first VC was awarded to Private Beach of the 92nd Highlanders while he was serving with the 55th Regiment (later 2nd Border Regiment). It was won during the Battle of Inkerman when he drove off several Russian soldiers who were attacking the wounded Lieutenant-Colonel Carpenter. A native of Dundee, Beach returned to the city where he died in 1864.

Ensign Richard Wadeson, 75th Foot, Indian Mutiny, 1857

Awarded during the operations in Delhi in July 1857. At the time men were collapsing from heatstroke and Wadeson saved the life of two privates who were in danger of being killed by mutineers. Born in Lancaster in 1826 Wadeson later became the Lieutenant-Governor of the Royal Hospital, Chelsea. He died in 1885 and is buried in Brompton Cemetery, London.

Private Patrick Green, 75th Foot, Indian Mutiny, 1857

One of the many Irish soldiers who served in the Gordons – he came from Ballinasloe in County Galway – Private Green was awarded the Victoria Cross at Koodsia Bagh during the operations in Delhi. Like Lieutenant Wadeson he showed conspicuous gallantry in driving off mutineers intent on killing a wounded comrade.

Colour Sergeant Cornelius Coghlan (also Coughlan), 75th Foot, Indian Mutiny, 1857

Another Irish winner of the Victoria Cross, Coghlan (or Coughlan) came from Eyrecourt in County Galway. Two acts of bravery were cited: on 8 June 1857 he rescued a wounded soldier and ten days later he encouraged a hesitant group of soldiers to attack an armed group of mutineers. He died in February 1915 in Westport, County Mayo aged 87.

Major George White, 92nd Highlanders, Afghanistan, 1879

George Stuart White was born at Rochester Castle, County Antrim and ended his army career as a highly decorated field marshal. He was awarded the Victoria Cross in Afghanistan in October 1879 when the 92nd Highlanders formed part of Roberts's field force which advanced on Kabul to depose Yakub Khan. During the operations at Charasiah he led his men into the attack, shooting the Afghan leader and forcing the Afghans to flee. He died in London in 1912 and is buried in his native County Antrim.

Lieutenant W.H. Dick-Cunyngham, 92nd Highlanders, Afghanistan, 1879

Awarded during the operations in Afghanistan in December 1879. Forced to retire from Kabul towards Sherpur, Roberts's field force came under siege and faced determined Afghan attacks. Aware that his men were wavering, William Henry Dick-Cunyngham drew his claymore and led a party of Gordons in an attack on the enemy's positions. A native of Edinburgh, he died from wounds sustained at the Siege of Ladysmith during the Boer War.

Private Edward Lawson, 1st Gordon Highlanders, India, 1897

The North-West Frontier was the scene of some of the bloodiest fighting for the British Army in the latter part of the nineteenth century. During a tribal uprising in 1897, the Tirah campaign, the Gordons formed part of a field force which attacked tribal positions on the Dargai Heights and succeeded in driving them off the high ground. Private Lawson was awarded the Victoria Cross for carrying two men to safety while under heavy enemy fire. A native of Newcastle-upon-Tyne, he retired there and died in July 1955.

Piper George Findlater, 1st Gordon Highlanders, India, 1897

Perhaps the most famous of all the regiment's Victoria Cross winners, Piper Findlater continued to play the pipes during the Gordons' attack at Dargai, despite being wounded in both legs. When he was invalided home to Scotland Findlater found that he had become a national celebrity and was invited to recreate the incident in music-hall performances. This upset senior officers, who felt that it was 'repugnant to military feeling' and Findlater was subjected to a good deal of criticism. After retiring from the army he took up farming in Banffshire but returned to serve in the Gordons on the outbreak of the First World War. He died in March 1942, aged 70.

Captain Matthew Meiklejohn, 2nd Gordon Highlanders, Boer War, 1899

At the Battle of Elandslaagte, fought on 21 October 1899, Captain Meiklejohn encouraged his wavering fellow Gordons to attack a Boer position by personally leading the assault. The kopje was taken but Meiklejohn lost an arm during the course of the fighting. He showed courage of a different kind in July 1913 when his horse bolted in Hyde Park and headed towards a group of children. Meiklejohn succeeded in turning it away, but he was thrown and died from his injuries.

Sergeant-Major William Robertson, 2nd Gordon Highlanders, Boer War, 1899

Robertson was awarded the Victoria Cross for his conspicuous gallantry during the latter stages of the Battle of Elandslaagte when he led a party to secure a Boer position. Despite being wounded and under heavy fire the Gordons held on under Robertson's leadership. He was later commissioned and died in Edinburgh in December 1949 in the rank of lieutenant-colonel.

Captain Ernest Towse, 1st Gordon Highlanders, Boer War, 1900

Awarded for two separate acts of bravery under fire. The first was at the Battle of Magersfontein when he carried a wounded fellow officer to safety. The second was at Mount Theba in April 1900 when an overwhelming force of Boers called on him and 12 other soldiers to surrender. Towse refused and led his men in a counter-attack which left him wounded and permanently blinded. He was later knighted, and died in June 1948 at Goring-on-Thames.

Lance-Corporal J.F. Mackay, 1st Gordon Highlanders, Boer War, 1900

During an engagement with the Boers at Crow's Nest Hill in May 1900 Corporal Mackay carried a wounded man to safety and tended to other wounded while under heavy Boer fire. He was later commissioned, reaching the rank of lieutenant-colonel, and died at Nice in France in January 1930.

Captain W.E. Gordon, 1st Gordon Highlanders, Boer War, 1900

William Eagleson Gordon was born in May 1866 at Bridge of Allan. He was awarded the Victoria Cross for his gallantry in pulling an artillery piece to safety near Krugersdorp while under heavy Boer fire. He remained in the army but was involved in controversy early in the First World War when 1st Gordons was forced to surrender to the Germans during the retreat to Mons. Later Gordon fought a libel case over the blame for the incident. He died in London in 1941 in the rank of brevet colonel.

Captain D.R. Younger, 1st Gordon Highlanders, Boer War, 1900

A native of Edinburgh, David Reginald Younger was killed in the same incident near Krugersdorp while helping Captain Gordon to rescue the British guns while under heavy Boer fire. He was mortally wounded during the action and is buried in Krugersdorp Cemetery.

Drummer William Kenny, 2nd Gordon Highlanders, First World War, 1914

One of the select band of military bandsmen awarded the Victoria Cross, Kenny rescued wounded men during the First Battle of Ypres in October 1914 and was also responsible for dragging two machine guns to safety. Born in Drogheda in Ireland, he died in London in January 1936 and is buried in Brookwood Military Cemetery.

Lieutenant J.A.O. Brooke, 2nd Gordon Highlanders, First World War, 1914

James Anson Ortho Brooke won his Victoria Cross at Fayet during the First Battle of Ypres in October 1914. Noticing that a large body of Germans had broken through the British lines, he gathered 100 men and led a vigorous counter-attack. Although his initiative stopped the Germans he himself was killed during the action.

Private G.I. McIntosh, 1/6th Gordon Highlanders, First World War, 1917

The only Territorial soldier to win a Victoria Cross while serving with the Gordons George Imlach McIntosh counter-attacked single-handedly a German position near Ypres in July 1917, killing two of the enemy and wounding a third. His initiative also resulted in the capture of two German machine guns. He later joined the Royal Air Force and died in Aberdeen in June 1960.

Lieutenant A.E. Ker, 3rd Gordon Highlanders, First World War, 1918

While attached to 61st Battalion, Machine-Gun Corps, Allan Ebenezer Ker and his machine-gun crew were surrounded during a German breakthrough near St Quentin in March 1918. Although surrounded and under heavy fire he refused to surrender until all his ammunition was spent and he succumbed to superior numbers of the enemy. He survived the war and died in London in September 1958.

Bibliography

Unless otherwise stated, extracts from soldiers' letters and diaries are in the possession of the regiment or are housed in the Imperial War Museum or the National Army Museum, London. Quotations are also taken from battalion and brigade War Diaries and other official papers which are housed in the National Archives, Kew.

BOOKS ABOUT THE GORDON HIGHLANDERS

Barker, Felix, *Gordon Highlanders in North Africa and Sicily*, The Bydand Press, Sidcup, 1944

Buchanan-Smith, Alick, *The Gordon Highlanders – Loos and Buzancy*, Aberdeen University Press, Aberdeen, 1981

Bulloch, J.M., *The Gordon Highlanders: The History of their Origin with a Transcript of the First Muster*, Banffshire Field Club, Banff, 1913

Cannon, Richard, *Historical Record of the Ninety-Second Regiment, originally termed The Gordon Highlanders and numbered the Hundredth Regiment*, Furnivall and Parker, London, 1851

Clerk, Rev. Archibald, *Memoir of Colonel John Cameron of Fassiefern*, Murray and Son, Glasgow, 1858

Falls, Cyril, *The Life of a Regiment: The Gordon Highlanders in the First World War*, vol. IV, Aberdeen University Press, Aberdeen, 1958

Fraser, David, ed., *In Good Company: The First World War Letters and Diaries of The Hon. William Fraser, Gordon Highlanders*, Michael Russell, Salisbury, 1990

Fraser, George Macdonald, *The General Danced at Dawn*, Barrie & Jenkins, London, 1970; *McAuslan in the Rough*, Barrie & Jenkins, London, 1974; *The Sheikh and the Dustbin*, Collins Harvill, London 1988

Gordon-Duff, Lieutenant-Colonel Lachlan, *With the Gordon Highlanders to the Boer War and Beyond*, Travis Books, Langley Macclesfield, 1998

Greenhill-Gardyne, Lieutenant-Colonel A.D., *The Life of a Regiment: The History of The Gordon Highlanders*, vol. III, 1898–1914, The Medici Society, London, 1939

Greenhill-Gardyne, Lieutenant-Colonel C., *The Life of a Regiment: The History of the Gordon Highlanders*, vol. I, 1794–1816 (92nd), David Douglas, Edinburgh, 1901; vol. II 1787–1881 (75th), vol. III 1816–1898 (92nd and The Gordon Highlanders), The Medici Society, London, 1929

Kennaway, James, *Tunes of Glory*, Longman, London, 1956

Lindsay, Martin, *So Few Got Through*, Collins, London, 1946

McCallum, Neil, *Journey with a Pistol*, Gollancz, London, 1959

McConachie, John, *The Student Soldiers*, Moravian Press, Elgin, 1995

Mackenzie, Captain David, *The Sixth Gordons in France and Flanders*, Rosemount Press, Aberdeen, 1922

Maclean, Rev. A.M., *With the Gordons at Ypres*, Alexander Gardner, Paisley, 1916

Miles, Wilfrid, *The Life of a Regiment: The Gordon Highlanders*, vol. V, 1919–1945, Aberdeen University Press, Aberdeen, 1961

Royle, Trevor, *Death Before Dishonour: The True Story of Fighting Mac*, Mainstream, Edinburgh, 1982

Rule, Alexander, *Students under Arms*, Aberdeen University Press, Aberdeen, 1934

Sinclair-Stevenson, Christopher, *The Gordon Highlanders*, Hamish Hamilton, London, 1968; *The Life of a Regiment: The Gordon Highlanders*, vol. VI, 1945–1974, Leo Cooper, London, 1974

OTHER BOOKS CONSULTED

Ascoli, David, *A Companion to the British Army 1660–1983*, Harrap, London, 1983

Barnett, Correlli, *Britain and her Army 1509–1970*, Allen Lane, London, 1970; *The Lost Victory: British Dreams, British Realities 1945–1950*, Macmillan, London, 1995

Barter, Richard, *The Siege of Delhi: Mutiny Memories of an Old Officer*, Folio Society, London 1984

Baynes, John, with Laffin, John, *Soldiers of Scotland*, Brassey's, London, 1988

Bewsher, F.W., *The History of the 51st (Highland) Division 1914–1918*, William Blackwood, Edinburgh, 1921

Brander, Michael, *The Scottish Highlanders and their Regiments*, Seeley Service, London, 1971

Brereton, J.M., *The British Army: A Social History of the British Army from 1661 to the Present Day*, The Bodley Head, London, 1986

Chandler, David, and Beckett, Ian, eds, *The Oxford Illustrated History of the British Army*, Oxford University Press, Oxford, 1994

Cromb, James, *The Highland Brigade: Its Battles and its Heroes*, Simpkin Marshall, London, 1886

David, Saul, *Churchill's Sacrifice of the Highland Division*, Brassey's, London, 1994; *The Indian Mutiny 1857*, Viking, London, 2002

Delaforce, Patrick, *Monty's Highlanders, 51st Highland Division in World War Two*, Tom Donovan, Brighton, 1997

Ewing, John, *History of the 9th (Scottish) Division 1914–1919*, John Murray, London, 1921

Fortescue, Sir John, *A History of the British Army*, 13 vols, Macmillan, London, 1899–1930

Hamilton, Ian, *Listening for the Drums*, Faber, London, 1941

Hamley, E.B., *The Operations of War Explained and Illustrated*, William Blackwood, Edinburgh, 1878

Henderson, Diane, *The Scottish Regiments*, Collins, Glasgow, 1996

Holmes, Richard, ed., *The Oxford Companion to Military History*, Oxford University Press, Oxford, 2001

Jackson, Bill and Bramall, Dwin, *The Chiefs: The Story of the United Kingdom Chiefs of Staff*, Brassey's, London, 1992

Keegan, John, *Six Armies in Normandy*, Jonathan Cape, London, 1982

Linklater, Eric, *The Highland Division*, HMSO, London, 1942; *The Campaign in Italy*, HMSO, London, 1951

Mileham, P.J.R., *Scottish Regiments*, Spellmount, Tunbridge Wells, 1988

Neillands, Robin, *A Fighting Retreat: The British Empire 1947–1997*, Hodder & Stoughton, London, 1996

Purdom, C.B., ed., *Everyman at War*, Dent, London, 1930

Roberts, Lord, *Forty-One Years in India*, 2 vols, Richard Bentley, London, 1897

Royle, Trevor, *James and Jim: The Biography of James Kennaway*, Mainstream, Edinburgh, 1982; *The Best Years of Their Lives: The National Service Experience 1945–1963*, Michael Joseph, London, 1986

Salmond, J.B., *The History of the 51st Highland Division 1939–1945*, William Blackwood, Edinburgh, 1953

Scott, Alexander, *Selected Poems 1943–1974*, Akros Publications, Preston, 1975

Stewart of Garth, David, *Sketches of the Character, Manners and Present State of the Highlanders of Scotland, with Details of the Military Service of the Highland Regiments*, 2 vols, Constable, Edinburgh, 1822

Stewart, J. and Buchan, John, *The 15th (Scottish) Division 1914–1919*, William Blackwood, Edinburgh, 1926

Strawson, John, *Gentlemen in Khaki: The British Army 1890–1990*, Hutchinson, London, 1989; *Beggars in Red: The British Army 1789–1889*, Hutchinson, London, 1991

Wood, Stephen, *The Scottish Soldier*, Archive Publications, Manchester, 1987

Younghusband, Sir George, *The Relief of Chitral*, Macmillan, London, 1895

Index

INDEX

INDEX

INDEX

INDEX